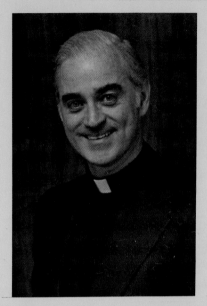

FATHER JOHN CATOIR is Director of The Christophers, a world-wide ecumenical organization that uses the mass media—radio, television and the printed word—to encourage people to take personal initiatives in making this a better world by raising public standards and carrying the burdens of one's neighbor.

Father Catoir recently completed a two-year term as President of the National Association of Church Personnel Administrators. He was ordained for the diocese of Paterson, New Jersey, in 1960 and completed his doctorate in Canon Law in 1964. He served in the Paterson diocese as the chief judge of the Marriage Tribunal for 10 years and as clergy personnel director for five.

Father Catoir was involved in parish ministry, both inner city and suburban, for 18 years. He is the author of four books and has written for numerous periodicals in addition to authoring a syndicated newspaper column.

ENJOY THE LORD

John T. Catoir, J.C.D.

<u>ENJOY THE LORD</u>
A Guide to Contemplation

Arena Lettres New York

This book is dedicated to the Holy Spirit who delights in teaching us how to dance.

Thus I survive
by skill, by luck
saved by art and grace

and I say
God
I delight in your work
I have seen you in stick and stone
my laughing God, Lord of the garden
Father of power over seed and root.

From moment to moment
invent my life
Lord of movement and change
invent me.

Gather the dusty sparrows of my days
hear them sing in your external branching.
Pain, exile, hunger
the bitter rains dripping through the walls
the house stripped
—I do not want a bed of roses.

Grass will grow
where beam upon beam, bone upon bone
stand now in measured connection.
—I do not want a bowl of cherries.

But, yes, invent my life, light
a passionate fire
a thing of blazing gold
and let me laugh in your joy
my laughing God
and leap in your rising
my Dancer!

—Catherine de Vinck,
A Book of Uncommon Prayers

Contents

Preface

Enjoy the Lord.

I agree with the fifteenth-century mystic Julian of Norwich that the highest honor we can give to God is to live gladly because of the knowledge of His love. That's why I wrote this book: to expand upon the idea.

After years of counselling priests, sisters, mothers, fathers and teenagers, I came to realize how difficult it is for most people to be joyful. Life isn't easy and there are always problems to weigh us down. On the other hand, we were made for joy and there is in us a human faculty tuned to God's inner life of total joyfulness. It is called the soul.

I have always believed that prayer should contribute to our sense of self-worth and inner happiness; it certainly should not diminish it. I am also certain that no one deliberately sets out to make himself unhappy. But there are some types of prayer programmed to do just that. I've come across a whole series of damaging ideas that are at the basis of much too much misery in the lives of good people. There is such a thing as good prayer and bad prayer and everyone should be aware of the difference.

I do not remember anyone ever teaching me how to *enjoy* the Lord. Perhaps it was supposed to be self-evident. If so, it wasn't to me. Only after years of struggle was I able to piece the puzzle together for myself. It isn't very profound, but it has helped me and enabled me to liberate many others from a path of joylessness. God wants to be loved and enjoyed by His children. He made them for an eternity of joy in heaven.

This book is an attempt to take the word "contemplation" out of the monastic setting and make it a household word. If you believe yourself to be a creature designed for love and joy and if you accept the Lord as unchanging Love, you can become a happy contemplative. "Man is the only young thing in the world. A deadly seriousness emanates from all other forms of life," says Eric Hoffer. "The cry of pain and fear man has in common with the other living things, but he alone can smile and laugh."

How true. We were made for happiness and we alone among created beings have the capacity for laughter. "My heaven has begun on earth because heaven is God and God is already in my soul" (Sister Elizabeth of the Trinity).

From our earliest days we were taught in religion class that our purpose was ultimately to be happy with God in this life and forever in the next. If only the teachers had spent more time telling us *how*. Saint Thomas Aquinas started in the right direction with this piece of wisdom: "The end of education is contemplation." I like the definition of contemplation that describes it as "the enjoyment of God." I do not believe the enjoyment of God should be left to monks and nuns in monasteries. *We* should have some fun too.

As I have said, in all my years of Catholic education, from kindergarten through the seminary and finally in doctoral studies, I cannot remember anyone teaching me how to enjoy the Lord. School always seemed to be a study mill, geared to "getting promoted" or "getting into a good college" or being able one day "to command a good salary." Serving God was always stressed and doing religious "things" was always encouraged, but *enjoying* one's life with God? Who taught that? Even today, I know hundreds of sisters and priests who do not accept the fact that they are contemplatives. They think it is a mystical gift given to those who have a contemplative vocation. In some cases it may indeed be that, but "enjoying the Lord" is the business of every Christian. It need not be done in hour-long sessions before a crucifix. It can be done while you're baking, riding the bus to work, going off to sleep at night or anywhere you like.

To contemplate you must first cultivate a real consciousness of your union with God. Consciousness of this union is essential. Fortunately, this union does not depend on your love for Him but, rather, upon His love for you. You may have to struggle to acquire virtue, but God's love is freely given, without any need for merit on your part. No amount of struggle or effort could make you worthy to attain it. His union with your soul is a free gift. All you have to do is believe.

The Lord God has always loved you, even in your sinfulness. He has desired to unite Himself with you before you knew Him. The Incarnation, Crucifixion and Resurrection of Jesus have been accomplished. Baptism has introduced you to supernatural life. God is with you now, as you read these words. He is always with you. The degree of your participation in God's interior happiness increases as you gradually open to His love, responding to it with gratitude and joy.

Most people become dissatisfied with their prayer life because they are not sufficiently aware of this marvelous reality. They may be too preoccupied with their failure to keep their good resolutions and then become discouraged. They have only cognitive knowledge of God's love; they lack appreciative knowledge. They do not realize how strongly God is united to their souls. It is not enough only to know theoretically that God is present. The Christian should consciously experience His Presence, responding to it with joy. Simple unforced, uncomplicated joy is the highest prayer. There are no methods of prayer that can guarantee the attainment of this joy. In fact, concern about methods tends to make a person self-conscious.

Enjoy the Lord is not just one more volume with a particular method of prayer. It is an attempt to help you go beyond methods and techniques. Part One deals with some of the mental and emotional obstacles that might impede your power to contemplate. For instance, a person cannot enjoy the Lord if he perceives Him as a distant or punishing God. Therefore, clear knowledge, which is faith, is the *sine qua non* of all contemplation.

Jesus taught us not to be anxious when we pray. Since the destiny of man is to enjoy God forever, it seems logical that we should enjoy Him *now*, without needless worry about reaching Him or "getting union" with Him. Jesus was trying to tell us something about our rightful inheritance of peace and joy. Saint Catherine of Siena put it well when she said, "All the way to heaven is heaven."

Prayer is not something to fuss about. The best of prayers flow easily from the heart, producing a kind of grave happiness because we are in contact with our Maker.

Part One is called "Prelude to Contemplation." Vocal prayer and mental prayer, though good in themselves, are only a prelude. Contemplation does not begin until all the words and thoughts stop. Contemplation is not thinking; it is more an experience of love. Any repentant sinner who knows that the Lord is unchanging love can contemplate. Even if that person is able to experience this happiness for only a few moments at a time, it is still a beginner's form of contemplation, and it is very pleasing to the Lord.

You may never be free of the human condition with all its distressing weakness and suffering in this life, but you can grow to love and enjoy the Lord. And He wants it. May God grant you increasing happiness in His love, both now and forever.

Part One

THE PRELUDE
TO CONTEMPLATION

With regard to the habit of conversing often with your
Divine Spouse, be confident that He will suggest to your
heart what to say. You are not embarrassed when you
speak to His creatures, why should words fail you when
you wish to speak to your God? Do not believe that
will happen to you: for my part, at least, I look on that
as impossible if you have acquired the habit of this
interior conversation with Our Lord.
                         —Saint Teresa, *Way of Perfection,* xvii

CHAPTER I

Starting from Square One

"I'm interested in learning a little about prayer," he said. *"I don't really believe much anymore. I've looked into a lot of religions, and most of them I don't understand."*

"Well, let's talk a little. Maybe I can give you a few ideas. Why are you thinking about this now?"

"It's just me. I'm not content with myself. I feel there's more to it than I know. I have some friends who are real believers and it seems to give them a lot of peace. There was also a death in the family. I think about death at times."

"A good friend of mine died just this week. It was a heroic kind of death. It took months for the cancer to take her and all the while she seemed to remain self-possessed, calm and even grateful. She had a deep prayer life and she had developed a grateful heart throughout her life. She's on my mind this week too. Her name was Jane. I'm sure she suffered a lot, but she seemed so much at peace. She taught me a lot about prayer."

"What do you mean?"

"Well, we're all so different, and yet so much the same. I'm not sure I could be anything like Jane in the piety department. She had her books and her beads and her statues. So much of her prayer style was personal to her."

"But you're a priest. Isn't that the way Catholics pray?"

3

"There is no single prayer style called "the way Catholics pray.' I don't think the members of any religion pray the same way. What I'm trying to say is that prayer is not necessarily bound to one style which is taught mechanically by a religious tradition. The overwhelming majority of the human race prays, and they all seem to pray differently. And yet, that's not quite right either because all of them *are* doing the same thing. If there could be one definition of prayer, perhaps the best one would be that it's living with God, responding to Him from moment to moment.

"Think about that. If spirituality means responding to God from moment to moment, then it must be a uniquely personal experience. The spiritual life of a person can never be exactly duplicated. We cannot copy. We can only live our own personal life with God. In a certain sense, there is no such thing as Franciscan or Buddhist or any other kind of spirituality. Saint Francis didn't follow Franciscan spirituality—he was Francis. Siddhartha wasn't a Buddhist—he was Siddhartha. Each one followed God in his own unique way. You can admire great spiritual leaders, but you shouldn't presume that the Lord is leading you in exactly the same way He led them. You are different and you are beautiful in your own distinctive way. Try not to copy anyone. Copying loses freshness, originality and spontaneity. You must be yourself. If you fail to do that you become a counterfeit of someone else. In other words, don't be too concerned about techniques."

"I'd really rather be myself anyway. I just don't know how to go about it, especially in praying."

"Being yourself isn't easy. Anyone even slightly familiar with the study of psychology knows that our conscious awareness of self is only the tip of the iceberg. We have deep unconscious drives that are also part of 'self.' So it is not simply a matter of telling people they ought to have a good opinion of themselves. You won't be able to have a good opinion of yourself if down deep you have some unconscious fear of yourself. The self-concept is important. We have been blessed because we believe God really loves us."

"Does he?"

"Of course he does. The greatest thing you can do for yourself is to believe in God's love and your own inner goodness."

"I do feel good about myself, but not always."

"But you should always have a good self-concept. A person may have done some bad things in his life and still be a good person. A poor self-concept is only an opinion. It is not a fact. The opinion you have of yourself is all-important in the spiritual life and you have to block out those negative opinions that distort your own reality. No one who has been told repeatedly by his parents or teachers that he's 'no good' or will 'never amount to anything' can hope to become good at prayer until he learns to love and respect himself despite the bad experiences of the past. Certainly he can't do it by attempting to become a copy of Saint Francis or any other saint. Some of our monasteries failed in the past because they were too quick to offer a program of holiness and not supportive enough in helping young people to appreciate their own self-worth."

"You don't mean you have to be psychoanalized before you can pray?"

"No, but it is essential that all of us learn to live with our shortcomings and value our own interior goodness. God loves us with an eternal, unchanging love. In spite of sin, weakness and failure, we are made in His image and He loves us."

"Down deep, I want to believe that."

"Well, then, believe it."

"It's easier said than done, Let's face it, there are things I like to do, and the Church says they're wrong. It makes me feel guilty."

"If you want to believe in God's love, chances are the grace of faith is already stirring in you. Sometimes you just have to take that leap in the dark. Faith in God's loving care does not depend on your ability to achieve perfection. Wherever you are now you can begin to love God."

"I don't feel I can do that very well, but I do feel that I would like to pray."

"All right, then, let's get back to prayer. Maybe a few simple ideas will help. In learning how to pray, try to remember two things. First, prayer is not so much what you *do*, as what you do *not* do. You have to stop running for a while to open yourself to God's Presence. It obviously helps if you know that His is a *loving* Presence. You have to relax your mind and body to some extent. Second, you shouldn't imagine that good prayer results in good feelings. God does not grade you according to your emotional feelings of solace and comfort. He wants the opportunity to offer Himself to you. He wants you to offer yourself to Him, to make a reasonable effort to put your entire life into His care."

"I like that, but how can you do it if you don't feel that God is listening?"

"You're putting too much emphasis on your feelings. There's a particular kind of knowing God that eliminates the need for continual slavish attention to your feelings. You don't have to do anything to win His attention. There are lots of people who pray anxiously and fretfully, as though God were in some distant place, preoccupied with many more serious problems. Just getting His attention seems to be the main problem for them. Lots of people spend a tremendous amount of energy just trying to get others to ask God to pay attention to their pleas. Believe it—God *is* listening.

"A calm dispassionate view of who God really is will dispel all this needless anxiety. He is as close to you as your own soul. He dwells in the intimate depth of your being. Your unique personality grows out of His Being and is rooted in Him. Just as a great work of art emerges from the mind of the artist, so do we all spring forth from God's mind. The original idea of you and me is still in His mind, though we are now free to move away from that idea if we choose."

"That's far out, but it's beautiful."

"You want to touch God. Touching God isn't a matter of exploration in the vast world beyond. It's more a return to the self, the deepest self. There's no need for any fuss about reaching out to Divine Life. We are always in His Presence. The instant we reflect on His abiding Presence in us, we become conscious of our union with Him. Once a person understands this, he has only to consider *who* it is that abides in him and with him. The Gospels tell us that God is unchanging love. There is present to us a lover who seeks to support and sustain us. If we let Him, God will guide and direct our lives."

"I really would like to try it."

"All you have to do is develop a taste for relaxed, open and honest communication. You need to learn to accept yourself and at the same time believe that God accepts you. Then you have gently to ask for the grace of holiness, the grace of transformation in Christ. Too few people really believe Christ when He tells them, "Ask and you shall receive." Usually, if they do take Him at His word, it is only for a brief time. Or they may ask for things that may not be proper for them at this time."

"That's the problem. How do you know anything for sure?"

"I admit it: Much of this prayer-talk is a mystery. There isn't an easy formula that contains all the secrets of finding a happy life with God. You have to learn to explore a bit more your own capacity for growth in the Lord. Saint Paul once said, "I live now, no not I, but Christ lives in me." Maybe the day will come when you'll be able to say such a thing and really mean it."

"Let's get off that for a minute. I'm willing to try anything but I'm not so sure I can get comfortable with the forms of prayer I see in the Church. There's a lot of ritual I don't fit in with."

"Ritual is the public prayer of the Church. But it's true: As Catholics, we have been taught traditional concepts even about private prayer. For instance, we pray on our knees before the Blessed Sacrament. We pray when we are attending Mass or making the Stations of the Cross. That kind of prayer involves a formal exercise, the performance of a ritual. But the word "prayer" refers to a much greater human experience than saying a particular set of prayers. I wrote a short book once, called *The Way People Pray* (Paulist Press). It covered briefly the ascetical approach of all the major religions of the world. Human beings are trying to say *Yes* to God, each in their own way. We really want to surrender to Him. We know we are creatures. There is nothing more that needs to be said."

"I pray better when I'm alone, but even then I feel unsure about it. What if you're the nervous type?"

"You're like a lot of others who are active and might be that type. You have to find the way of lifting your mind and heart to God that best suits you. Leave the monastery schedule to the monks and look to your own life pattern to find a way to pray every day. The first thing you have

to do is learn *to relax.* Try to let yourself go and just talk
to God in your own words. You've probably done that a
thousand times over. Most people really *do* pray."

"I can relate to that."

"You've probably been praying a lot more than you're
willing to admit. It really is simple and uncomplicated. He
is there with you. God is always present. His presence means
infinite, unchanging love. It is you who must remind yourself
of His presence; take the time to go to Him and do not
measure your success or failure. Not everyone is a contemplative in the traditional sense of the word, but a lot of
people have come to terms with themselves and their busy
lives, and they do pray."

*"I know a few who are into transcendental meditation
and it seems to help."*

"Yes, it does help a little, and do you know why?"

"No."

"Because those who succeed at it have committed
themselves to a routine and they stick to it. TM really isn't
prayer. It's the first step to prayer. Prayer is communion
with God. TM puts the necessary halt to everything else
and releases the mind from the cares and strains of daily
existence, but of itself it is not actually prayer."

"Why not?"

"It doesn't claim to be. It isn't supposed to be reli-
giously oriented. Although there are vestiges of Hindu
worship in it, most of the people who practice TM are
into it strictly for the practical results: peace, serenity,
relaxation."

"What's wrong with that?"

"Nothing. It's great. But we're talking about prayer,
aren't we? I mean, a hot bath is peaceful and relaxing, but
you couldn't call it prayer. TM is just a tranquilizer."

"Are you against it?"

"No, but I do have a little problem with the candle-lighting ritual before the picture of the chief guru. But if you throw that out and just use TM as a technique to quiet your nervous system, I think it could be very therapeutic. I think that because 'stopping' and 'relaxing' are absolutely necessary in order to pray deeply, TM is a great beginning."

"I'd like to pray deeply."

"Well, it is a holy desire to want to pray. There are many forms of prayer that are good in themselves but deep prayer, contemplation, is special. It is the way of many people who strive for holiness. Some aren't able to give themselves to it because they don't make it a priority item. They just don't give time to it. I can understand that. Life can be hectic. For most Americans the idea of stopping everything for twenty minutes or more is hard to get used to. What they don't seem to realize is that contemplation is enjoyment. To contemplate is to enjoy God. It's easy."

"Easy?"

"Yes. In itself prayer is easy. Just forcing yourself to take the time to do it can be difficult. That's one reason why I think TM has helped a lot of people, at least those who have stuck to it. They pay a lot of money to learn the technique but only a few of them are faithful to it. When they are, it's seemingly effective because they have become convinced that they have to stick to their schedule and stop everything. They go into a trance at least once a day. For me, the trance isn't enough. It's mere emptiness. I want to be filled with the glow of God's loving presence. I have that enjoyment with me all day, but most especially when I pray deeply."

"What if you don't know for sure if God exists?"

"Without that knowledge, you don't really pray. I mean, you can't really communicate with God while you're saying, 'Dear God—if there is a God—help me to save my soul, if I have one.' "

"But what if that's the best you can do?"

"All anyone can do is the best he can. Saint Augustine gave us some excellent advice when he said, 'Do what you can do, and pray for what you cannot yet do.' I wonder, though, if it really *is* the best you can do."

"Maybe I should pray to be able to believe in God."

"That's not a bad idea. Someone might say it's dumb, but the truth is it might be all you can do right now. It *is* something."

"It sounds a little like self-hypnosis."

"It isn't. Do you know why? Because God is really there. Even if you can't imagine what He's like, you know He must be there. The world, the stars, the universe—they all have to have an explanation. Something doesn't come from nothing. God is real."

"I wish I could be convinced."

"The only way is to just let it happen. Belief, or faith, is a leap in the dark. Maybe you have to understand your own mental conflict before you are free to give up your fear of being a fool."

"How do you mean?"

"Have you ever noticed the way the imagination and the intellect can work against each other? Sometimes one just interferes with the other. For instance, if you go to a funeral, you may hear the widow say, 'I can't believe he's dead. I just can't believe it.' Notice the word 'believe.' What she means is that she can't picture it. Imagination requires pictures, images. She can't imagine what life will be without him because she can't picture her home without him in it; she can't imagine the breakfast table without him being there. She feels a conflict. Her mind is confused. Her intellect tells her he's dead. He's there in the casket, but she still says, 'I can't believe it.' Her imagination is working against her reason.

"We do the same thing with God. We know intellectually that something doesn't come from nothing, but we can't picture God, so we conclude that He isn't there. I believe in God, not because I have an idea of Him in the abstract and not because I can picture Him. I believe because I know it by some inner knowledge. He has touched me in some way."

"Maybe we say we don't believe because we don't want to believe."

"*You* said that. But you're right. Maybe it has something to do with the will as well. I'm sure some people don't believe in God because they can't imagine Him or picture what He is like. Others understand that the idea of a Supreme Creator really makes sense and yet they withhold belief. That's more crafty, more self-deceptive. They really don't want to believe in God. They're afraid that the act of belief itself will force upon them a relationship they do not want."

"How so?"

"Down deep, they are convinced they can't live a good moral life or they simply would rather not try. They're trapped in their own weakness and they think that going to church or praying is hypocritical, like telling the world that they're holy and good. Since they don't feel that good, they don't like to pretend they are. They really don't want to be involved with a God who may complicate their life in this way. They prefer other things. They may want the freedom to seek after money, power, sex, whatever."

"I don't think I want power, but I do want some of those other things. Sex and money aren't bad."

"No, they're good in themselves. The challenge is in

using God's creation according to His will. Human life is not easy, but try to believe that God wants to give us strength and comfort to live it happily. He isn't there to compound our guilt. In fact, it's because we need relief from guilt that we turn to Him in prayer. I have a prayer I want you to read. Maybe it will help you. Even if you can't say you believe, just try reading it once in a while— and thinking about it. Just imagine that God is talking to you."

You do not have to be clever to please me; all you have to do is want to love me. Just speak to me as you would to anyone of whom you are very fond.

Are there any people you want to pray for? Say their names to me, and ask of me as much as you like. I am generous, and know all their needs, but I want you to show your love for them and me by trusting me to do what I know is best.

Tell me about the poor, the sick, and the sinners, and if you have lost the friendship or affection of anyone, tell me about that too.

Is there anything you want for your soul? If you like, you can write out a long list of all your needs, and come and read it to me. Tell me of the things you feel guilty about. I will forgive you if you will accept it.

Just tell me about your pride, your touchiness, self-centeredness, meanness and laziness. I still love you in spite of these. Do not be ashamed; there are many saints in heaven who had the same faults as you; they prayed to me and little by little, their faults were corrected.

Do not hesitate to ask me for blessings for the body and mind; for health, memory, success. I can give everything, and I always do give everything needed to make souls holier for those who truly want it.

What is it that you want today? Tell me, for I long to
do you good. What are your plans? Tell me about
them. Is there anyone you want to please? What do
you want to do for them?

And don't you want to do anything for me? Don't you
want to do a little good to the souls of your friends
who perhaps have forgotten me? Tell me about your
failures, and I will show you the cause of them. What
are your worries? Who has caused you pain? Tell
me all about it and add that you will forgive, and be
kind to him, and I will bless you.

Are you afraid of anything? Have you any tormenting,
unreasonable fears? Trust yourself to me. I am here.
I see everything. I will not leave you.

Have you no joys to tell me about? Why do you not
share your happiness with me? Tell me what has happened
since yesterday to cheer and comfort you. Whatever
it was, however big, however small, I prepared it.
Show me your gratitude and thank me.

Are temptations bearing heavily upon you? Yielding to
temptations always disturbs the peace of your soul.
Ask me, and I will help you overcome them.

Well, go along now. Get on with your work or play,
or other interests. Try to be quieter, humbler, more
submissive, kinder; and come back soon and bring me
a more devoted heart. Tomorrow I shall have more
blessings for you.*

"This prayer may help you grow in what is called
mental or conversational prayer. It will also help set the
stage for contemplation. Contemplating is simply gazing

---

*Anon.

upon the Lord, without words, or thoughts or symbols. It is essentially the spiritual enjoyment of God.

"In a word, if you desire to delight the loving heart of your God, be careful to speak to Him as often as you are able, and with the fullest confidence that He will not disdain to answer and speak with you in return. He does not, indeed, make Himself heard in any voice that reaches your ears, but in a voice that your heart can well perceive. He will then speak to you by such inspirations, such interior lights, such manifestations of His goodness, such sweet touches in your heart, such tokens of forgiveness, such experience of peace, such hopes of heaven, such rejoicings within you, such sweetness of His grace, such loving and close embraces, in a word, such voices of love, as are well understood by those souls whom He loves, and who seek for nothing but Himself alone." *

---

*Saint Alphonsus, *The Way of Salvation and Perfection* (Brooklyn: Redemptorist Fathers, 1926) p. 408.

CHAPTER II

Confidence in Personal Prayer

1. GOOD AND BAD PRAYER

Some people expect themselves to be perfect and feel discouraged when they fail. But no one can be his own judge in these matters. The phrase "good prayer" implies that there is such a thing as bad prayer, which is true. But too often we judge our success or failure at prayer on a false basis. It is not the way we *feel* about our prayer that makes it good or bad, but its effect, its fruits. As the Gospel puts it, "By their fruits you will know them."

The Pharisees prayed constantly and they seemed to feel good about it, yet Jesus rebuked them because of the hardness of their hearts. They were saying to themselves, "Thank God I am not like the rest of men!" That is why He called them hypocrites. On the other hand, bad feelings about your prayer does not mean it is actually bad. The saints often write about their spiritual dryness, their distractions and temptations during prayer, yet their lives were extraordinarily fruitful.

You really can't judge your own spiritual fruitfulness, and I'm going to tell you a parable to help explain what I mean.

An old lady lived on a large estate with many servants. Every day she would rock for hours in her parlor, reading the Psalms. She faithfully attended Sunday services and generously supported the Church with her donations. Her wealth came from the rent from hundreds of apartment units she owned in the poor section of town. She never visited her properties, but demanded that her agents be strict in collecting the rent. Many a poor family that could not meet the monthly bill was thrown out on the street. As she rocked and soothed herself with peaceful prayer, she seldom gave a thought to the source of her income or to the fate of the evicted families. When she did, she appeased her conscience with the thought that people should learn to meet their obligations. Then she would pray, "The Lord is my Shepherd, I shall not want." Often, she would thank God for blessing her materially and spiritually. She would feel good about her prayer life.

In the same city lived another woman, a widow who taught the fifth grade. She had thirty-six children in her class, a particularly active and demanding group. Every day was draining on her energy. By the spring of the year she was near exhaustion, but she pushed on against her weariness, without missing a class. Partly because of her weakened state she developed an ear infection that made her slightly deaf. Her fellow-teachers, jealous of her success with the children, took advantage of it to taunt her. She did her best to ignore them, but when she got home in the evening she would often cry alone. It was her custom to pray every night for a half-hour. Her head would be full of pain. Although she had to fight temptations of spite and revenge and believed her prayers to be of little worth, she kept on praying.

Which of these two women was the more pleasing to God? If you know the answer, you will begin to understand the meaning of the distinction between good prayer and bad.

2. GOOD PRAYER DOES NOT DEPEND ON GOOD FEELINGS

Simply because you feel good about your prayer doesn't mean it is pleasing to God. Simply because you think everything is wrong about your prayer doesn't mean you are failing to please Him. Most people expect too much of themselves. Everyone has difficulty with prayer. Even the saints at times found their efforts at prayer personally frustrating. Human beings are so easily discouraged. When you allow this to happen, you are being unkind to yourself and your prayer becomes less supportive than God intends it to be. He wants you to feel confident about Him. His love is eternal and unfailing. Being kind to yourself has a great deal to do with establishing the proper attitude as a permanent mind-set.

The Lord is kind and tender with you. Can you dare to be anything but kind with yourself as you travel your inner journey? Be at peace with yourself and live gladly because of the knowledge of His love. Good feelings are not always necessary in a love relationship. Love transcends feelings.

3. GOOD PRAYER IS NOT ANXIOUS

You worry sometimes about your weaknesses and occasionally you get depressed over your failures. It's only normal. Sometimes you complain that your prayers are not answered. Lots of people do the same thing. You have to carry on, but the burden becomes heavier when you blame yourself for not being worthy enough. A Christian is not called to be a worrier. All you have to do to please God is to make a sensible effort to be good. A charitable heart is your goal and you don't have to be perfect to be charitable.

Most human beings have programmed themselves since childhood to become somebody special. Consciously or unconsciously, they seem to seek their own glory. Their earliest fantasies involve the attainment of greatness. They have an "idealized" self in their minds and, for better or worse, they are always striving to attain their dream. When they face themselves as they really are they become sad. Perhaps you have had this nagging dissatisfaction with yourself, the feeling of being a "nothing" because you're merely average. But ask yourself: Do I really see myself as being better than average? If you think you are, then everything you do will be affected by your above-average expectations. Your prayer will be shaped by this self-idealization.

You are a human being. You can never be free of imperfection. You can never be an angel. You have to accept your true self: your face, your body, your sexuality, your allergies, your ulcers; all your weaknesses and your strengths. You must accept yourself. Jesus loves the sinner. You must do the same. You waste too much energy feeling discouraged for not being the Superman or Wonderwoman you think you should be.

The first thing you have to learn if you are to pray well is to stop condemning yourself because you feel inconsistent, unworthy or guilty. In fact, you have to stop judging yourself at all. There are lots of reasons why you are far from perfect. Given your parents and grandparents, the unknown ancestors you've had, the troubles you've experienced and the times in which you've had to live, you are doing amazingly well. You're an average person, not a special case.

Your body is an ordinary one, not a machine exempt from the laws of wear and tear. A whole range of disorders accompany you through life: skin problems, indigestion, bunions, nervous disorders, blurred vision, overweight, etc. All of them can be discouraging for one who dreams of attaining some superhuman status of success and fulfillment. When we say "Glory be to God" we should be turning over our hunger for glory here and now to Him.

By middle age most people feel that time is running out; that they haven't done anything of any great importance; that they are in fact declining in every way, particularly on the spiritual level. It is a common human experience, but remember, feelings are not facts. You are called to be a loving person and you have already achieved that goal to some degree. Expecting too much of yourself and everyone else is a form of vanity. Vanity urges a person to conjure up grandiose images of what he or she might hope to be. Face, figure, disposition and virtues are all idealized. Failing to achieve glory, one tends to be disappointed with self. This is more obvious in teenagers, who often pretend to be something they are not. Naturally the prayer of such good but misguided people will assume a certain unreality. They will be using God to achieve their dream and when it becomes clear that He does not grant every wish they become worried.

How can prayer have any real meaning if people use it as a technique to actualize a false self-image? Religion means doing the will of God not one's own. Before getting down on yourself for not realizing your dream of perfection, find out if your dream is from God. Don't waste nervous energy praying for something that God doesn't want for you. God never asked anyone to be great. He loves human beings, ordinary people, and that means people who bite their nails, people who exaggerate, people who are overweight, people who smoke too much, people who have erotic thoughts, even people who steal or murder. God despises sin, but never the sinner. You must learn to see yourself as the Lord sees you, through the eyes of love. It is the work of the devil to fill you with the thought that you are worthless, rejected, despised. Don't believe it. Don't be anxious about your faults and failings or about God's love for you. It is infinite, personal and eternal. The Lord said, "Be not anxious." God loves you just as you are. He knows how to make you His instrument. He knows how to bring you to His own radiant glory. In fact it is He who seeks union with you.

4. GOOD PRAYER BUILDS ON HUMAN WEAKNESS

As human beings we are very prone to ordinary weaknesses. We are called to an extraordinary vocation, called to struggle against evil and worldliness. But in that struggle we cannot become disheartened because of our humanity. Most people are stuck with a whole set of unseemly traits and failings that hold them back from being their dream-self. The discouragement that comes from such self-inflicted tyranny is needless worry. Weakness is not an enemy, it is a friend. By the power of Jesus Christ your weakness can become your strength, but you must understand in the light of the Lord's teaching.

The weaknesses that humiliate you are usually the average weaknesses of human nature. As long as your heart strives for goodness, the spirit of holiness is working in you. Your mind is controlled by the Holy Spirit when you want to do what is right. That's why Jesus was patient with Peter when he went to sleep on the night before the crucifixion. "The spirit is willing but the flesh is weak." One of the great principles of the spiritual life is "Know thyself." Do not mistake performance for holiness. Holiness is a mystery and a gift. There have been many saints who lamented their weakness but nonetheless were among God's most precious instruments.

In 2 Corinthians, Saint Paul gives us a glimpse of how it works. He suffered from some problem that seemed to distress him and give him a sense of failure and humiliation. The experts differ on what it actually was. Some think it was sexual temptations; others, a physical disorder. It doesn't really matter. He describes his own state of soul: "And indeed for fear that these surpassing revelations should make me proud, I was given a sting to distress my outward nature, an angel of Satan sent to rebuff me. Three times it made me beg the Lord to be rid of it, but He told me, 'my grace is sufficient for you for my power shines forth more perfectly in your weakness.'" With that insight, Paul was converted into accepting himself and his weakness (which he no doubt felt was unworthy of his idealized self). He finishes this passage with the words "More than ever, therefore, I delight to boast of my weaknesses that humiliate me, so that the strength of Christ may enshrine itself in me." Paul is not saying, "Hooray, I am weak and I choose to do nothing about it," but rather that he rejoices in God whose strength stands by him so that in spite of his weakness God will draw from him a rich harvest of abundant good fruit.

Do not be afraid that by following Paul's example you will become lax, self-indulgent and spiritually weak. Left to yourself, you are already lax, self-indulgent and spiritually weak. Maybe you feel you are not going to do much better, but certainly you are going to keep on trying. Once you know that and accept the ambivalence of the human condition, you will learn to depend on our Lord Jesus Christ who uses the weak things of the world to confound the strong. His power needs your self-acknowledged weakness and dependence.

"God gave to some animals the speed of flight; to others, claws or wings; but He has so disposed man that He, God Himself, is his strength" (John Chrysostom).

The goal of this team effort (God working in you, through you and with you) is the fulfillment of the Supreme Law: LOVE. His idea is to get you to stop worrying about your distractions at prayer, your temptations and failings; to get you to step out into the world around you and pay attention to others. Allow Him to love and minister to them *through you*. Your weakness is no obstacle to this. He loves it. Consider the twelve apostles when He first picked them. Through the ages He has in fact chosen weak instruments for His work. He can do marvels through weaklings if they can only relax and believe He is using them to bear rich fruit.

One serious obstacle to love of neighbor is smug self-satisfaction (like the old lady in the parable). Be glad that God is your strength. Because of this knowledge you can, like Saint Paul, even go so far as to rejoice in your infirmities, in your aches and pains, moral imperfections and spiritual lapses. The Lord loves you just as you are. He loves all sinners even though He wants them to become holy and sinless. He alone can make you into a dazzling white knight or a woman of destiny. Your glory is *His* business, not yours. Turn it all over to Him and your transformation in Christ will begin. You will be empowered to bear good fruit. This act of turning everything over to the Lord in itself is a powerful prayer.

5. GOOD PRAYER PROMOTES SELF-RESPECT

All prayer is vain if it does not help you to love. To love, you must accept yourself, and to accept yourself, you must understand that you are an ordinary human being.

Even though you may fall from time to time you know that God loves you. He needs your hands, your voice and your heart to minister His saving love to others. Self-acceptance is the first sign of healthy and proper self-love. From this starting point it becomes reasonable to accept and eventually to love your neighbor. You cannot deal charitably with the faults of someone else if you cannot accept your own faults. Conversely, you can better accept others with all their failings once you've come to terms with your own. Until you accept yourself, nothing grows. God never changes in His love for you, but unless you realize that, your prayer will be full of frustration. If you want to please God you have to be grateful for what He gives you. Teach yourself to have a good attitude about your own body, however imperfect it may be. Those who hate their body attack themselves unfairly. Even if it is misshapen every human body is still an amazing creation.

It is not enough for you to know that there is nothing dirty or evil about the human body. You must appreciate that it is good. The physical complex of organs, functions and sensations is good. Like all the wonders of nature, your body is good—meaning beautifully designed, integrated in its operations, useful, well-conformed. But it is also good in a much more profound order. Man is more than a tree or an animal and the very essence of this higher order is the fact that he is an heir to the Kingdom, a child of the Promise. It is to your body that resurrection has been promised.

It is not enough to say that you love your own body. You must *realize* that you love it. You must offer to God the homage of your being just as you are. It does not please Him to hear you complaining all the time about the gifts He has given you.

I once knew a woman who was very unhappy. Believe

it or not, the root of her misery was that she hated her own heart. It was a sick heart and from childhood she had been forced to limit her activity. She resented her heart and, therefore, her body, and her own person. By God's grace I was able to convince her that she had life only because of that poor little organ which was working so hard to help her enjoy God's gifts. Eventually she saw the light, accepted her heart with love and was freed from the terrible mental affliction of self-hate.

If you do not love your own body you are not going to pray well because prayer is essentially a grateful disposition in God's presence. It is a work of love. Most books on prayer begin and end with the love of God. But you can only love God when you are free to love self and neighbor. Pleading for favors and begging for help, as many do, is certainly prayer—and the God of mercy and love hears all prayer—but He wants you to become less anxious about your needs and more ardent about becoming a warm and loving human being. The Lord must grow weary of our pleading for an apple when He wants to give us an orchard. Try to listen to His love. He touches every aspect of human life. Prayer is a work of love not merely because we are trying to love God but because He is, in fact, loving us here and now, always and ever. He sends us signs of His love over and over again. Once you become aware of this, not merely as a matter of belief but as a lived experience, you have passed through your apprenticeship. Such a gift can be prayed for, but never demanded as a right.

If Jesus, the Lord, could speak to you right now, He might very well say: "Why are you worrying about your prayer? I am always here. I am unchanging in my love for you. Because of your repentance, your sins are no more; my forgiveness washes them away. Think no more about the past except to glorify my mercy. The future is in my control. Do not be afraid. You are not growing lax simply because you accept yourself as human. If you fail to achieve the level of perfection you have designed for yourself, be at peace. I have better plans for you, but I need you to be humble, pliant and dependent on my power. I will answer your prayer for personal sanctity in my own good time. Allow my design for you to be the measure of your progress. It is not my will that you become perfect according to your own plan. The Pharisees strived for perfection and look what happened to them. Many of them called me an evil-doer and had me put to death. It is my will that you please me by loving others well, by loving yourself well. In this you will be loving me. I am asking quite a lot, I know, but unless you examine your conscience on the way you treat others, on the way you love those around you, you will be blinded by self and constantly preoccupied with your own limited understanding of failure and success."

6. GOOD PRAYER PRODUCES A SWEET SPIRIT

You can read any book you like on topics such as religious life, religious perfection, gospel spirituality, mystical revelations or ascetical theology. They all come down to the same thing: *charity*. If your prayer could move mountains but you do not have charity, it is only vain and empty babbling. A sweet spirit is filled with charity, patience and kindness, not only toward others but also toward self. You cannot be kind to others if you cannot be kind to yourself.

Bitterness is not sweetness of spirit. How many bitter people have you met who try to have an active prayer life? They may say prayers, but their spirit is dissatisfied. Bitterness, resentment, hatred—these things are not from God. It is usually true that bitter people have been hurt by someone. Hurt may grip the spirit for a time, but by God's grace it will never be allowed to turn to bitterness. Jesus was not bitter, not even on the cross. Bitterness sours the human spirit and produces a flood of sins against charity. The real Christian is determined to love his or her neighbors no matter what they have done. Jesus taught us to love even our enemies. The will to love is the beginning of a sweet spirit, the beginning of real prayer. Even if you are filled with bad feelings toward someone, you can still forgive him.

If you want to correct a sour spirit and bring it sweetness, here are a few ideas. Granted, it won't be easy if you have been wounded by someone's failure to love or, worse, by someone's hostility, but there is always grace. The longer you nurse your wounds, the longer you postpone your own liberation. To become a new creation: (1) Pray for the gift of a loving heart. (2) In times of distress call frequently on the name of Jesus. (3) Believe that you are solely responsible for your thoughts and actions and blame no one else for your present state. If you have suffered a great reversal or humiliation do not blame your parents, your superiors, your upbringing or your environment, but, rather, realize you made your own choices. If you must face a tough decision, face it and make it. (4) Realize that pain, sadness and unhappiness often came to you because you did not take prompt action to do the right thing. (5) Admit your errors, correct them and promptly forgive yourself. (6) Pick yourself up and begin again.

Some people always blame others for their problems. They then become hostile, push others aside and hurt them, thus becoming in themselves what they despised in others. They do not realize it, but they are seeking first their own glory instead of putting God's glory above themselves. A sweet spirit is not like that. Even a hardened criminal can be changed, with God's help.

"Charity overcomes a multitude of sins." In spite of

your weakness God gives you the power to love. You need
only ask. Prayer is both the asking and the receiving. It
calls forth the energy to be a forgiving person not because
it may make sense, but because Jesus asks it. That's why
bitter people can and indeed *must* pray. It isn't sweetness
of spirit that produces prayer, it is *prayer* that produces
sweetness of spirit. Pray for the gift of a loving heart and
thank God often for what He already has poured into you.

7. GOOD PRAYER IS FAITHFUL

We have been taught rather traditional concepts about
prayer. For instance, you pray when you are on your knees,
in church or beside your bed at night. Prayer is understood
as consisting of some formal exercise, the performance of
some ritual or another. But it is really a much more varied
human experience than the traditional formulas suggest.
Each person may go about it differently. For some, a book
is used as spiritual reading and the thoughts awakened by
the writer serve as the impetus for lifting the mind and
heart to God. The reader drifts away from the book as a
feeling of God's loving Presence is awakened in his heart.
That is called affective prayer. In this state there is no
need for words or books. There is merely one simple act
of wonder in which the entire spirit is filled with God's life.
Time passes without being noted; in fact, it has no meaning.

The experience of prayer is not always like that, however, even for those in contemplative monasteries. If the
rapture of affective prayer was easily attained on a daily
basis by all who try there would be little need to encourage
people to pray. Unfortunately, it is not. Let's be honest,
we are not always attracted to prayer and, because there is
effort involved, we pretend we can't get to it.

There are, at times, long periods of aridity when we

feel only numbness and inertia, but these are moments when we meet God in desolation. Don't be discouraged with your lack of consistency. Even the saints suffered such things. "Sometimes when I am in such a state of spiritual dryness that not a single good thought occurs to me, I say very slowly the 'Our Father' or the 'Hail Mary,' and these prayers suffice to take me out of myself and wonderfully refresh me" (Saint Theresa of Lisieux, *Autobiography*, chap. 10).

God loves you just as you are. Your inner turmoil is itself acceptable to Him as an act of love. Prayer can be done in a million ways: Enjoying life is prayer, enjoying music is prayer, enjoying work is prayer, giving is prayer, receiving is prayer, life itself is a prayer.

Yet, while all this is true, it is important to set up some definite time pattern of prayer. A freely chosen discipline of daily prayer is a good way to insure that you will gather yourself together on a fairly regular basis before the Lord, whether you are in peace or turmoil. It is important to be faithful in prayer, but faithfulness to a formula does not mean that you will always feel the same way about your prayer.

There are problems that interfere with good feelings at prayer. If it is undertaken early in the morning you may have to contend with sleepiness. If it is begun in the middle of the day, when the adrenalin is worked up, distractions bombard the inner quiet. If the evening is chosen, a kind of weariness ensues and gives the impression that one is half-asleep rather than praying. All of these things can lead a person to conclude that praying is useless "for them." But this is foolish. You must accept your humanness even at prayer.

Part of the problem is that most of us are frantically busy. Pope John once said that Americans have a difficult time praying because they do not know how to relax. A very wise man was he. There can be no enjoyment of the Lord without a spirit at rest.

The first thing to do when you begin is to relax. Try to become comfortable. Let yourself go. When a feeling of relaxation comes over you, let yourself drift gently into a deeper level of consciousness. Your awareness remains very much intact as you prepare to commune with God. He is there and you are there. God is always present to you. His Presence means infinite, unchanging love. Trust Him. Be with Him. Receive from Him. Imagine Him caring for you. Do not measure your success or failure. You really should not judge yourself in these matters. Just go to Him.

Can such a labor, day after day, be pleasing to God? Yes. But even if the whole time is filled with inner noise and distraction there is the joy of conscious offering of self to God. He does not grade your prayer, giving you an *A* when you feel cozy about it. You must avoid all such delusions and just learn to relax. Make the effort to use your moods themselves as your prayer, even if they are uncomfortable, instead of trying to regulate your prayer by your moods. Sooner or later you will understand that daily prayer is an experience of quiet joy. The time for prayer is the time when you transform and transpose your daily experience, lifting it up to the Lord. He in turn delights your heart by giving Himself to you.

> It would appear that before the close of the Middle Ages the masters of the spiritual life did not deem it needful to appoint a fixed hour each day for meditation. At the present day, however, this custom is not only advisable, it is absolutely necessary. Such is the hurry and bustle of modern life, such the multiplicity of interests and of social obligations, that it has become almost impossible for men to lead a life of union with God unless they reserve one tranquil hour for Him in the early

morning, before the whirlwind of their occupations
carries them off, covering their souls with its blinding
dust and deafening them with its noise.

—Cardinal Mercier, *Conferences*

8. GOOD PRAYER IS PATIENT

Be patient with God. He could have given you what
you asked anytime He wanted to. If you want some new
grace and your prayers have not been answered, do not
allow your confidence to be undermined. There could be
many reasons for it. Examine your motives more carefully.
Try to please God, not your own vanity. God knows your
need. He sometimes withholds His gifts for His own reasons.
It is not given to us to know everything all at once. We
can only know a little at a time. What we do know,
however, is that God deals with us very gently. Even His
withholding is done with great love.

The gifts will come in God's good time. Saint Paul
puts it well in Romans 5: "These sufferings bring patience,
as we know, and patience brings perseverance, and perseverance brings hope, and this hope is not deceptive because
the love of God has been poured into our hearts by the
Holy Spirit which has been given us."

Be patient with yourself and your neighbor. Each time
you pray you have to slow down the works of the human
brain. Come to a halt and be still. It isn't a bad idea, either,
to keep in mind the advice of Saint James in Chapter 1 of
his Epistle: "Pure unspoiled religion in the eyes of God
our Father is this: Coming to the aid of orphans and
widows when they need it, and keeping oneself uncontami-
nated by the world."

In brief, your prayer life requires the awareness that

you are striving realistically to please the Lord on many levels. Do not expect yourself to give a superhuman performance all the time. You'll never be able to. The quest for the sublime will only cause a sense of failure and frustration in you. So you must learn to be patient. The key to prayer is in knowing that He wants to work in and through your humanness. He does this on His own schedule, not yours. You cannot plant an acorn on one day and expect to go out and sit in the shade of an oak on the next. Be patient.

I will reveal to you a secret of sanctity and of happiness:
If every day, during five minutes, you are able to quiet
your imagination, to close your eyes to the things of the
senses and your ears to the rumors of the earth, to
enter within your self, and there, in the sanctuary of your
baptized soul, which is the temple of the Holy Spirit,
thus to speak to this Divine Spirit:

> Holy Spirit, Soul of my soul, I
> adore Thee.
> > Guide me, strengthen me, console me.
> > > Tell me what to do, give me Thy
> > > orders,
> > > > And I promise to submit
> > > To whatever You desire of me
> > > And to accept everything
> > > You allow to happen to me.
> > > Let me only know Thy will.

If you do this, your life will flow happily, serene and
consoled, even in the midst of pain, for grace will be
proportioned to the trial, giving you the strength to
bear it; and loaded with merits, you will reach the
gates of Paradise.—Cardinal Mercier, *Conferences*

9. GOOD PRAYER IS JOYFUL

Since God is Love, it is His joy to be with you. When you grasp this, you will begin to know the personal joy of being with Him. Prayer is a joyful experience.

It is often said that your work is your prayer, but this is only partially true. Certainly you can make your work an offering to God, but offering anything can only be a part of your prayer life. If you do no more than offer your work you will not experience God's response to you. If you hope to keep a clear mind and bear good fruit in your life, you have to find the time to be alone with God to enjoy His Presence. Your praise and thanksgiving can be a warm and happy expression of this joy. Silence is also a beautiful expression of joy.

You need to speak to God, but you also need to *listen* to God's life. You need to receive *consciously* more and more of His power and tenderness. You receive God by forgetting yourself and listening to Him. Even though you have needs, you do not always have to barge in upon God's Presence with your litany of requests. He may not talk to you in a human voice, but you will know Him. His eternal, unchanging love is there, flowing to you now and forever. Prayer is the act of adverting to this reality of love. It is enjoying all that God wishes to give on a particular day.

Prayer is food for the spirit. The absence of this food can breed doubt, fear, confusion, sin and all the effects of sin. So prayer is receiving something essential to your life. You do need God and His Beatitude so that you may learn the meaning of spiritual joy.

10. GOOD PRAYER IS LOVING

You need to realize and appreciate the fact that God's love is always available. You do not have to think about it.

He has not left you alone, uncared for, comfortless. Compare His Presence to the water in your kitchen tap. It is there all the time, but when you are thirsty you must bring the water forth. In a similar way, you need to draw forth God's love by being aware of and enjoying it. For most people, this is an intellectual effort. Christians concentrate on Jesus, who is the very image of the Father, the loving Son of God who came to save and comfort us. He gave us His name to use when we approach the Father. But it is possible to love God without conceptualizing. Ask the Father in Jesus' name to increase Divine love in you here and now, thank Him for His goodness, and then love Him.

You must, of course, believe and trust that God is responding. He promised it, didn't He? Begin to feel His strength; enjoy the new confidence coming to you and thank God in the very process of receiving this help. As you listen or receive Him praise Him as Jesus did so many times in His own life, on good days and bad. The love of God knows no limits, no boundaries, but you must receive it consciously. In the act of praising God you are enjoying God's Presence. Praise Him for all that He is. Praise Him in His Glory, for the beauty of the universe. Praise Him for all that He has done for you. Return again and again to the fountain of His love for the refreshment you need to live a joyful Christian life. All praise be to God!

> Do not be astonished at the difficulties one meets in the way of mental prayer, and the many things to be considered in undertaking this heavenly journey. The road upon which we enter is a royal highway which leads to heaven. Is it strange that the attainment of such a treasure should cost us something? The time will come when we shall realize that the whole world could not purchase it.

The first thing I wish to discuss, as far as my limited understanding will allow, is the nature of the essence of perfect prayer. For I have come across some people who believe that the whole thing consists in thought; and thus, if they are able to think a great deal about God, however much the effort may cost them, they immediately imagine they are spiritually minded; while, if they become distracted, and their efforts to think of good things fail, they at once become greatly discouraged and suppose themselves to be lost. I do not mean that it is not a favor from the Lord if any of us is able to continually meditate upon His works; and it is good for us to try to do this. But it must be recognized that not everyone has by nature an imagination capable of meditating, whereas all souls are capable of love. I have written elsewhere of what I believe to be the reasons for this wandering of the imagination and so I am not discussing that now; I am only anxious to explain that the soul is not thought, nor is the will controlled by thought, it would be a great misfortune if it were. The soul's profit, then, consists not in thinking much, but in loving much.

—St. Teresa of Avila, *The Book of Foundations*

CHAPTER III

Removing Guilt and Fear

Dealing with guilt feelings can be a serious problem. You will have a new confidence in yourself, a new level of love, peace and simplicity of life, once you learn how to rid yourself of needless guilt. To grow in this spirit of peace, you must learn to reject the inner voice that condemns and criticizes your every action, the voice which frightens you day after day with petty worries. This voice is not from God.

You are probably not unlike the rich young man in the gospel who followed Christ. He was a good man, but he was not a saint. Remember him asking, "What must I do to be saved?" And Christ answered, "Keep the Commandments." "But I have done this since childhood," he said. And Christ replied, "If you would be perfect, sell all you have and give the money to the poor and come follow me." The young man is never mentioned again. He found Christ's challenge too much to bear. Perhaps he felt guilty in his later years for failing to follow Him more perfectly.

There are times when guilt feelings are authentic and therefore helpful. But sometimes they are merely nervous symptoms. In either case they are not dangerous in themselves because Christ's healing love is always present to us, helping us to overcome the fear of rejection and disapproval. Just above the psychological sea of worry caused by guilt there is a layer of calm that we can attain at will if we have the faith to reach for it. By going consciously to the Lord, by praying, we can free ourselves from the neurotic demands that cripple our potential for joy and peace. We can draw God's own peace down upon us when we offer our present state of mind to the Holy Spirit. For instance, if we are angry with someone, we do not allow ourselves to stew in that anger. We immediately call upon the name of Jesus and ask for help, offering the anger to Him, to be transformed by His power. We then pray for that person who angers us. This is a discipline that must be practiced. Too many people linger in a negative mood without even thinking of the Lord. No matter what the negative emotion may be, we can act against it through Christ's power. If we are depressed, we do not linger in that state. We give it over to God and consciously receive an inflow of peace and joy from Him. This is particularly true when guilt feelings come upon us. Whatever mood we may be in, whatever temptation we may feel, if it is negative we do not choose to accept it. We give ourselves over to the Lord. We thank Him for freeing us and we praise Him for His marvelous works in our life.

We must also recognize that we are capable of sin, great sin, and that this is a reality that points up our precarious, fragile, spiritual existence. If we feel sorrow over past sins, it is futile and foolish to sustain that mood. We have been forgiven. Guilt feelings serve a purpose if we examine them, discern them to be authentic and ask for the forgiveness of the Lord. Feelings of guilt that drive us to repentance are meant to be temporary. But if they persist in the lives of people who are making a real effort to be good they should be banished. Freeing oneself of guilt can be an act of worship in itself. It frees the mind to praise God for His great goodness.

The powers of darkness are at work in the world to an alarming degree, but we are not left alone undefended. People who no longer fear evil, or hardly even recognize it, are the ones to be pitied. Evil is real. We must retain our knowledge and fear of evil and our sense of guilt if we do wrong. True guilt can be helpful, but for one purpose only: to lead us to correct our ways. Once that decision is made guilt has done its work. It is really a blessed pain which can open the door of repentance.

False feelings of guilt, however, must be rejected. Scrupulosity, which is an extreme case of neurotic guilt, is something that does no one any good at all. It only causes needless anxiety. We should always pray for a mind filled with light, peace and joy. Sometimes the exorcism of neurotic feelings is found in prayer. God does not want us to stew over our imperfections. He wants us to have a healthy, happy frame of mind. Believe this. He truly does. If a person wants to please God he should begin by learning to live gladly because of His love. This is why God created us. By getting outside of our own private world of negative feelings we can become free to be more loving human beings, free to be what God intended us to be.

The only way we are able to respond more sensitively to the needs of others is by taking care of our own basic needs and by learning to pay less attention to our false ones. The people who always put all their own needs first are the ones who care the least about the needs of others. Those who put their own excessive needs in the background are the ones who care most about the needs of others. It is that simple. What is not simple, however, is the ability to distinguish between real needs and excessive, or false, ones.

The mother who sacrifices herself for the family in a million little ways is often taken for granted because others in the family, especially teenagers, tend to put their own needs first. It's not easy to keep on giving and worrying about others when they take you for granted.

Fathers have needs as well as responsibilities. They must work, sometimes for long hours in highly competitive settings, in order to support the needs of the family. This may, at times, create a conflict with basic personal needs. The good father always strives to live up to the high ideals of his position. More heroic parents actually ignore their own legitimate needs for the sake of their children. A bad father, conversely, fixes his attention on his own needs. He sees little of the needs of those in his immediate household and nothing of the needs of those outside—in his town, his country. Usually, he justifies his approach to life and appears to have no guilt, no insight into his selfishness. In these cases guilt would be a marvelous remedy, if only the person could respond honestly.

Some people are more self-giving than others. They are the ones who, through God's grace, are able to forget themselves more and more. They are eager to go about doing good. They inconvenience themselves. They suffer the risk of abuse, ingratitude and neglect even though they can be easily hurt by others. They can become immune to criticism or hurt, but they never enjoy it. At times, their own feelings of guilt well up. They may think they are being selfish because they find that they, too, have needs that must be met. They struggle to deny such needs and continue to respond to the needs of others, which often leads to resentment. While this is going on the problem is compounded by those who try to make them feel foolish for placing the needs of others above their own. Temptations arise and they dream of escaping, which only causes further guilt and anxiety.

All of this is a waste of energy. We do what we can. We serve as best we can. The Lord sees our efforts and He blesses them. He looks with pleasure on those who suffer this way. He loves them with an infinite love because they are among His most noble creatures. They are His children from the beginning, the ones chosen for special care. They are striving and He loves them for it. He knows their needs: He supports them and guides them. He wants them to grow in the knowledge of His love. In this pursuit, guilt is of no help at all.

God is Love. That is the most important truth we can ever learn. Christ taught it by His life and example. He knew His Father's Love. He taught His followers that this love touched them as well.

An upright life is beautiful but it is a struggle. Today, any discussion of guilt as a blessing and a source of strength, valid though it is, needs to be balanced by the truth of God's unchanging love. We can use guilt as a signal, an interior impetus to move on to something higher and better, but it should never obliterate the truth that God loves all of us, even the most hardened criminal, with an infinite love.

Archbishop de Provencheres Le Tubet writes some consoling words: "When I make my examination of conscience, rather than remembering my sins I prefer to remind myself of all the love Christ has had for me during this particular day, or morning, or during the time since my last confession. If one looks at oneself, although it is perhaps not all bad, all the same it is not very brilliant; whereas if one looks at the love of Christ for a soul, or for His Church, one can only sing a hymn of thanksgiving. . . . The things that are going badly are the work of the devil, and that is why I prefer one not to have too many scruples about one's sins; one has to think of them only so as to see God's forgiveness" (*Jesus Caritas,* Summer, 1974).

Imagine what that advice could have done for the

countless millions who have suffered severely with guilt feelings. The emphasis here is not on the sin but on the love of God. Our greatest problem is not so much our sinfulness but our inability to accept ourself as we are, body and spirit. There are some very fine people who do not actually sin, not seriously at any rate, but who dislike themselves intensely. They are displeased with their own body, annoyed with their weaknesses and certain that everyone else disapproves of them, including God. The failure to love and accept yourself—your own body, your own personality, even if less than perfect—is a deliberate failure in gratitude. We are called to have a grateful heart in all things.

The Archbishop continues: "We should always think about what God does, and not about what the devil does. The things that are going badly are the work of the devil; and the things that are going well are the work of the Holy Spirit. Adding things up I think that there are more things going well than going badly. Much more attention is paid to the noise of walls that are falling down than to the sounds of seeds which are growing. We must be attentive to the sound of the seed which is growing, all the extraordinary work of the Holy Spirit in the Church, all this transformation."

What is important is the way we allow the Third Person of the Trinity to work in us. The Holy Spirit is working in the Church today through countless individuals. Numerous prayer groups are springing up all over the world and many people are deepening their prayer life, especially young people. As the Archbishop says, "It is they who will be coming to the seminaries and the novitiates before long."

There have been many events that have debilitated the moral strength of our nation, our cities, our towns and our families. But to dwell on them is only to reinforce their impact on our lives. We need to remind ourselves of Christ's promise to draw good from evil. We are not weakened but strengthened by adversity. We are not losing but gaining in the pursuit of our final goal. Part of this strength is in the will to count our many blessings and the capacity to see the good beneath the surface of confusion and noise. Instead of cursing what we lack in ourselves and thereby increasing our distress, we ought to thank God always for what we *do* have.

There are subtle pains in life that do not attract any notoriety but hurt nonetheless: a misunderstanding with a relative or friend; a separation from someone dear; the absence of faith or spiritual concern in a son or daughter; the fear of losing one's job; the fear of failing in an important undertaking. These are the pains that gnaw away at one's hope. But there are ways to keep the burdens of life from undermining our confidence. There's a toughness within us that can meet these challenges, an untrembling center that will not be overcome by pain and sorrow. There is grace. Grace is God's gift to us to help us cope with the burdens we bear.

We have Christ within us and His Presence gives a dimension to our experience that transcends all human emotion, all human pain. A believer must truly believe this. Misunderstandings will be healed; separations eventually will be resolved; those who do not now see His light will have their eyes opened if we pray for them. There is time; there is grace. God accepts us as we are and He sends us our daily bread. We need only acknowledge His gift and be glad. Guilt over the past and fear of the future can dissolve if we turn immediately to Jesus. We are reminded by the Lord not to coddle these needless worries. "Be not anxious about tomorrow; sufficient unto the day are today's troubles." We are not left poor and helpless by Jesus. There is grace, always and ever. The Lord will bring us through today's problems just as He has before in all the yesterdays of our life. But needless anxiety, needless guilt, is not in the Divine plan. We will see more clearly the hidden purpose of our life if we accept the fact that guilt is meant to be banished by God's forgiveness.

Reality is hard. The Lord never promised it would be easy, but He did show the way. In fact, He *is* the Way and by believing in His acceptance and love we can weather any storm, overcome any obstacle, open any door. If, in the course of events, His superior intelligence allows the laws of nature to cross what we consider our best interests, we must trust and not waver in that trust.

The Lord suffered humiliations, pain, betrayals, even death. As a man, He wept in the pain of loss, at the prospect of His own death. He felt the sting of abandonment and rejection. He knows well what we suffer because He suffered it all, but He triumphed over sorrow and death. Those who have the eyes to see claim that triumph in their own lives; they choose to be confident because of His love. Trust is what He asked of his followers.

"Come to me all you who labour and are overburdened and I will give you rest. Shoulder my yoke and learn from me, for I am gentle and humble of heart, and you will find rest for your souls. Yes, my yoke is easy and my burden light" (Matt. 11:28-30). There are some who hear these words and expect instant magical relief for their pain and sorrow. If disappointed, they quickly move on to seek relief elsewhere. They are like the stony ground on which the seeds fell but took no root. Others see in this gentle teaching of Jesus a much deeper message, one touching their very life and destiny, and rightly so. This gospel message goes to the heart of our religious life. If we understand it properly it can release enormous power for us. Christ does not waste words, nor does He deceive us. He is the Way. He is the Lord. These words are true.

Most people battle their way through life not asking the Lord what He wants, but determined to achieve their own goals and objectives. They don't really know how to turn it all over to Him, how to surrender everything. They push and pressure to get what they want and they learn the hard way that life does not easily bend to their will. Even so, they cling to their battle plan, convinced they are on the right path, following the right way. They do not really ask the Lord to show them what He wants. They may think they do but, in fact, they only turn to Him to get His support in carrying out their own plan. They want Him to fit right in with their ideas, to make their dreams come true. However understandable, this is not Christianity.

Christianity is concerned with the Father's will, just as Christ Himself was. Experience teaches us that ups and downs, sickness and death, are part of every life. Jesus did not come to exempt us from the human condition. He came to bring us home to heaven, to save us from eternal damnation. He says "Follow me . . . I am the Way." It is we who surrender to His way. Our life is not really our own to do with as we please. It is we who learn to follow.

Christ shouldered the yoke that was placed upon Him in a spirit of joyful acceptance, not in a mood of grim resignation. What we need to appreciate is that the same Spirit that enabled Him to do this is in us right now. It is the Spirit of God which gives us the strength to surrender. If we ask we will be enabled. My own experience has taught me that it is highly efficacious to have others pray over you and with you to receive this grace. The Charismatic Movement has taught me this.

"Shoulder *my* yoke . . . and you will find rest for your soul," says the Lord. It is His plan that enables us to bear good fruit. Our plan of life will be good and worthy only insofar as it conforms to His will. If guilt serves a purpose it is only to steer us to safety. Beyond that it can be neurotic. A spiritual advisor might be a help here. "Seek and you shall find; knock and it shall be opened to you."

Do you ever ask the Lord what it is He wants of you? Are you really Christian enough to put Jesus first in your life; to make Him the Lord of your future; to pick up your cross and follow Him? Are you terrified that He may ask something foreign to your present values and tastes? Are you afraid to give up your sin, your inappropriate involvements, your dark feelings? Most Christians like to think of themselves as being in tune with Jesus, but their spirit is not full of joy, peace and love. They are filled with self-recrimination, resentment, hostility, fear. They cling to these negative feelings, too proud to surrender everything to Jesus.

Do not expect to be given the peace of Christ or have your yoke made easy and light if your yoke is your own daily creation. The yoke God promises to make light is of Divine creation. He tells us to shoulder that yoke. Under it you will find your peace. Through your commitment to Jesus you draw the power you need to move on to His glory. Indeed, His yoke is easier and lighter than any you could fashion for yourself. "Come to me," says the Lord, "and I will give you rest." I personally believe that everyone who has ever asked God to help them attain this rest, this peace of heart, this self-acceptance, eventually will be granted their wish, even if they fail miserably for a while. God's power is infinitely stronger than man's weakness or obstinacy.

In his book *Man's Search for Meaning*, Viktor Frankl tells the story of a young Jewish girl who was imprisoned in a concentration camp during the war. Frankl is a psychiatrist who, while a prisoner himself, observed those men and women who managed to survive the horrible ordeal of wartime prison camps. Apart from mass executions, starvation and pestilence were the common causes of death. Some managed to survive in spite of years of disease, torment and degradation.

The author had known the Jewish girl as a child. She was born slightly demented but was attractive in appearance and well cared for at home. Though raised in a Jewish home, she showed little interest in religion. In her early teens she became notoriously promiscuous. German soldiers made easy use of her body. She was cocky and unaffected by the talk and ridicule of the townspeople. As Hitler's stranglehold over Germany gradually began to show its sinister anti-Semitic character, she was arrested. With all her so-called friends in the military, no one lifted a finger to save her.

Frankl discovered her a few years later in a concentration camp. She was emaciated, wasted and near death. Her mind was totally gone. She recognized no one and was thrown in a cell with others who were mentally deranged. They were given little care and barely enough to eat. Her room reeked of the stench of excrement and she was covered with her own filth. Everyone in the cell was totally out of contact with reality, living in a private dreamworld. Frankl watched the girl and observed how she would periodically raise her arms to heaven and mutter some prayers in Hebrew —prayers she no doubt had learned in her early youth. Oblivious to everything around her, she did only one rational thing: she prayed. One day, while in the very act of praying to God, she fell dead.

She is a symbol for so many others who have been crushed by forces greater than themselves. What stands out so remarkably is her spirit, dormant for years, covered with layers of abuse and neglect, stunted by mental weakness at birth. The only vestige of humanity she retained was her yearning for God. When all contact, all human hope had vanished, when reality itself was pushed aside, her spirit lived and raised its sights to the Almighty One, calling on Him for help, forgiveness, salvation.

We need have no hesitation about the power of God's mercy. Infinite mercy is so far beyond our comprehension it would be folly to describe it. Today that girl is somewhere in heaven, safe, clean, redeemed. She is happy with God. I have no doubt of it. Her's was a baptism of desire.

How her mother and father must have been tormented by her behavior. In becoming a prostitute, she totally abandoned any semblance of respectability. In her promiscuity she drifted into some mysterious darkness which created an enormous chasm between her and her parents, but their early training was still part of her being, right to the end.

It seems that no moment of love and care is ever wasted. This is a very consoling thought for parents who are disappointed by their children. It is a great mystery how, in time, God's life emerges. Even at the very end, there is time. God's eternal mercy envelops our temporal order. Time as we know it has no meaning in God's eternity. Today's prayers keep alive those tiny flames of light in ourselves and in those we love. They reach out to loved ones, through God's mercy, across the limitations of time and space. They become part of the all-consuming fire of Divine love and eventually achieve their objective. This is why Christianity is a religion of hope. This is why we are all Easter people and *Alleluia* is our song. We are not overcome by guilt. We rise above it and become a new creation.

Do you believe this? If you do, there is no need to explain further why God is meant to be enjoyed.

CHAPTER IV

Observing How Others Pray

Learning from the experience of others sometimes helps us to understand prayer. I have collected some letters from people who were kind enough to share their experiences with me. They have developed their own rhythm and style. Do not imitate—you can't be someone else—but it helps to listen to others and see if they have achieved joy and peace. I'd suggest you consider this something of a "private tour," then choose the ones you like best. Try to discern if these people are enjoying God.

The first letter is from a friend named Jane. While she was growing weak with terminal cancer I asked her to write about her feelings about it.

"I have been asked to write about my 'personal thoughts and reflections since learning that I am dying.' The truth of it is that I do not think of myself as dying anymore than anyone else. When I realized that I was seriously ill, I knew that my life would end, but I have always known that. The real thing is that none of us knows exactly when. Now, although I know I am not well, I do not feel particularly sick. At first, when I was having radiation treatments and was under various medications in an attempt to find a right one for me, I was weak, in pain and not very alert. When I was talking to old friends on the telephone I often found myself sorrowful, for it was as though I was making my farewells.

"But my most immediate and spontaneous reaction was one of gratitude for a long and healthy life, enriched with innumerable blessings. Coupled with this was a desire to do whatever good I could in the remaining time and to make preparation for the death that was to come. I have no idea when death is likely to be.

"Gratitude was the strongest force. I had lived a long life and with God's help had tried to make it a useful one. My life had been filled with blessings. I had enjoyed excellent health and much happiness. My children, whose father had died when they were very young, were now adults and no longer needed my physical care nor material support. In addition, they were leading good and useful lives. Also, I was blessed with grandchildren who were being brought up in a good and happy home, with loving, hard-working parents who were interested not only in guiding their own children but also in helping others. I had known God's love and felt His closeness and guidance many times. What an abundance!

"And yet there was more. My parents had been exemplary, and my brothers and sisters and I had been brought up in a home replete with spiritual and material blessings. As my life progressed I had known many fine, extraordinary and wonderful people and had been enriched by their friendship. So, as my mind drifted back over the years, I could see only the great goodness of God showered upon me in every way.

"In thinking of His goodness, I realized again what failings had been mine and I asked His pardon again for all the ways I had failed, all the times I had sinned. I regretted my infidelity more than ever because I knew of His constant love and care. I marvelled at His great love.

I had known it and His providential care and had depended on it for years.

"I had asked to be carried in His arms and I had permitted myself, so far as I could understand, to be guided and directed by His Holy Spirit, to be placed where He would have me, to undertake the work He opened to me. It was not great. It was not wonderful. It was the simple work of everyday, of the marketplace, lovingly and faithfully undertaken in His service. I had no other way to show my gratitude and love for His care.

"There were times when I was tempted to regret that with all the gifts of intelligence, health, good home-life, education and friendships with holy and exemplary people, I did not mature to greater success and prominence, that I did not do great things for God. This was not a new thought. But the spiritual reading I had done over the years had warned me that this could be pride, so I put aside ideas of greatness unachieved, accepted my smallness, my obscurity, and prayed again that God would use me in any way at all because I loved Him and knew that He knew me better than anyone. He knew what was best.

"And so I can accept my illness as just another disclosure of God's will for me. My life's professional work had drawn to a natural close. I had been wondering how I might give myself to some work in His service and had begun to undertake volunteer work, feeding the sick in a hospital. My illness, suddenly disclosed, made it impossible for me to continue. I accepted His will without question and rather with gratitude for making it so clear.

"Because I have such complete trust in His providence, built up over the years by the recitation of a prayer to Divine Providence, I accept whatever happens, knowing it can be for my good if used properly. My desire is to give myself in whatever way I can to His service. While I have a

few hours a day of fairly comfortable physical activity, I like
to attend Mass and to meet occasionally with friends, trusting in God's Providence to use these meetings for His pur-
poses. I try to be thoughtful and kind and loving, but I fail
often. It is always my sense of gratitude that fills me with
compunction for my many failings. How can I be so
thoughtless and unkind when God is so good to me?

"I like to think that I am a reservoir of His love,
and that as a street vendor might pass out a cup of cool
water to a passerby, I may use some of the love He has
given me to refresh my neighbor.

"So, my illness is just another reason for gratitude.
I have been warned that my life may be drawing to a close.
This is a great blessing and I can now knowingly make
ready. I was able to receive the Anointing of the Sick in the
presence of my family during the celebration of Holy Mass
in my home. What peace and joy to receive these final
blessings in full possession of one's wits and surrounded
with the presence and love of one's friends, children and
grandchildren.

"How long will these final days stretch out? I have no
idea. Each day is a gift from God and an offering to Him.
For years I have lived in His love. I believe in Him and all
He has told us of Himself and His kingdom. I shall die
some day. I pray that He will sustain me at that dying
time so that I will be faithful to all I believe. As I have
trusted in His Providence all my life, I trust Him now. As
he loves me, He shall take me into His kingdom, and the
love in which I now live can only be increased.

"And so my personal thoughts and reflections are
happy ones: gratitude for God's innumerable blessings,
with this recent one of being given time to prepare, a desire
to be of whatever service I can be and complete trust in
His continued Providence for me."

Jane died a couple of months after she wrote this and I read her message at the funeral Mass. If such a serene spirit can come from prayer, how can anyone fail to make prayer a part of his daily life?

ॐ

A saintly priest who was trained in his spirituality long before the Second Vatican Council showed evidence of a more formal approach to prayer. He is to be admired for the discipline in his prayer life. Perhaps not too many will be able to imitate him exactly, but the goal of our prayer is not in imitating others; it is simply to enjoy God and abide in His will.

"I prefer, whenever possible, to be in the presence of the Blessed Sacrament. So I go into chapel and sit where I can see the tabernacle.

"My preparation often consists in reading a short passage from the Gospel; frequently it will be the selection from the Lectionary for the reading of the day, but at special seasons I switch. For instance, during Lent I try to meditate only on the Passion. But let's say that I were to read the selection for Saturday of the Nineteenth week of the year (Matt. 19:13,15) about the apostles chasing the children away from Jesus and His admonition: 'The Kingdom of God belongs to such as these.'

"Once I have the topic, I try to create the scene by mentally visualizing Jesus and the apostles and the children. I enter into the scene, so as to be in contact with Jesus, either as a spectator or as a participant. Then I spend some time thinking about this 'mystery' and trying to get absorbed in Christ. Generally, a theme emerges: the gentleness of Christ with the children, His correction of the disciples, His love of innocence, the naturalness of children or the beauty of simplicity. This theme I try to reflect upon, without agitation.

"There is sometimes a kind of mental petition, such as, 'Jesus, teach me to be natural in your presence.' There is a kind of quiet waiting for the Lord to take the initiative. Very often I am aware of the closeness of Christ in the sense that I would say I experience Christ. The attitude is one of listening to the Lord—a somewhat passive waiting for the Lord to speak, if He is going to.

"During the prayer there will often be a sense of gratitude, of admiration, of adoration, of happiness or of contrition. If I do not experience such sentiments, I will make an act of love or of gratitude or of sorrow or whatever else the occasion demands. I think of this as affective prayer and often prolong it merely by repeating the Holy Name.

"Near the end of the prayer period I try to determine what resolution is appropriate for that day. I formulate it and ask our Lord to help me practice it. Finally, I try to fix the scene of the meditation deeply in mind, so that I can recall it during the day whenever I wish to become recollected, whether at formal prayer (The Office) or just by a quick ejaculation."

ह✤

The following letters from lay people speak for themselves. Each is a little different, but all are sincere descriptions of a personal approach to prayer.

"I start my day with the morning offering to the Sacred Heart. I 'talk' to our Lord and our Lady all day, with little aspirations; pray to the poor souls and at bedtime I make a good act of contrition. Then I say the Act of Consecration to Christ the King. This prayer, to me, is the most complete prayer—when you meditate on it it covers almost everyone who might need prayer. I then say the Memorare. It is one of the prayers I tried to teach my children to say each day, so each night I say it, offering it to our Lady from any one of the children who may not have said it that day for any reason.

"My final prayer for the day is: 'My Lord and my God, I offer Thee the Sacred Heart of Jesus, with all its suffering, all its merits, to expiate the sins I have committed this day, to purify the good I have done badly and to supply for the good I have neglected to do this day and all of my life.' "

ह∾

"This is roughly how I pray:

" 'God, I thank You for everything You have done for me today. I thank You for my eyesight, my ability to walk (I will be eighty-nine in April), eat and drink, read and write, play my harmonica and use my typewriter. I thank you for my good food and my nice room. Because You are always with me, I need to be in close communion with You always. Please guide me along the paths of good living and help me to throw away my bad habits and replace them with good ones which will please You.

"Thank You for my good health, and thank You for creating my cells, atoms, glands and organs, for they are working hard to keep my body in the shape you created it to be. Please bless them. I thank my cells, *a, g* and *o,* for their good work, and I know God is blessing them. Because

You are with me, every day in every way I am getting better and better. I am not aging, but I am prospering, and I want to prosper so that I can help the needy.

"Thank You for what You have done for me in the past, and for today, and for what You will do for me in the future, for I know You will never forsake me. Today will be a day of freedom to do all things which will please You; a day of love, empathy for all living things; a day of hope that very soon all peoples will worship you so that peace on earth will be possible.

"Please bless all my friends, acquaintances, relatives and any enemies I might have; also all those who may not like me for any reason. And please safeguard them when driving their cars. And those who have lost their loved ones. Please bless those who are ill, or depressed, please heal their bodies and minds. And those You have healed in answer to my prayers, please, Lord, help them to keep well now that they are well.

"I thank You for bringing peace to the peoples of Nigeria, Pakistan and India, and for the end of fighting in the Middle East and Vietnam and Korea. Please Lord, bring a lasting peace among the Arabs, Egyptians, Syrians and Israelis, peace wherever there is strife.

"God, I thank You for hearing me, and for Your everlasting kindness to me."

ફ~

"I love to pray and I pray at any time, in any place, in any way. My day starts off with the reciting of formal prayers of the Church. Through these, I've come to know about many great Christians—not from the sense of their history but because of their feeling and their love of God and His people. The Memorare was the most meaningful as

I prayed it for six months to insure that our child (the third one) would survive his birth. Many others followed—those to St. Joseph, St. Thomas Aquinas and St. Ignatius Loyola; the Prayer Before a Crucifix; to St. Francis of Assisi and many, many more. More than once I have suddenly realized that a part of my life has been transformed by one of these prayers, and just as suddenly, that that prayer no longer seems special to me and another suddenly speaks to my heart. I've come to recognize this as a way Jesus is leading and teaching me the direction He wants my life to take.

"As time has gone on, I've been lead into many different prayers and ways of praying. I've sat in silence just staring at the cross and Jesus until I thought my heart would break. I've sung for joy—shouted Alleluia! And then, at times, I've cried for joy, too, realizing how much I love Him and He loves me. I've found myself wording my own prayers to our God in ways that at times have astounded me. I've knelt, sat, laid down, stood up, squatted; but it never seems to matter, Jesus always listens. Sometimes it's with my arms crossed over my chest, sometimes with them limp at my side, at other times, with them extended to heaven, yearning to reach and hold my God.

"The Rosary still holds a special place of prayer for me and has acted most often as a spring prayer for a variety of other forms of prayer during and after completing it, which at times has taken me an hour or more to do. My car has become an especially good place to pray and traffic and gas lines don't seem nearly as long.

"At times, I've just sat or stood in awe looking out at my Father's beautiful world and let Him speak to me. I guess this is the best prayer—letting Him speak to me. That, and the constant repeating of the name 'Jesus' all through the day. What a beautiful and powerful name it is.

"All in all, the most exciting thing about my prayer is its infinite variety and excitement as the Spirit leads me from and through one form to another."

ट&

"No doubt we all have our own way of praying. I will express mine as simply as I can.

"Three years ago I consecrated myself to Jesus through our Blessed Lady and now when I pray and ask favors I go to her first and ask her to intercede for me. I used to become so uptight when I had problems and I just pleaded that my prayers would be heard. One morning, I was crying and talking to my husband before I went out to Mass and he said to me: 'You are going to Mass every morning and if you do not have faith in God that He is going to hear you, then why go to Mass?' It hurt me deeply at the moment, but what he said was a turning point for me to have more trust. As the years have passed since my consecration, I have acquired a wonderful peace. I can cope with much more and I know that when He is ready He will answer me and grant the things we need to help us to go on.

"I am a Legion of Mary member and this too has been a wonderful inspiration to me. I have found that in doing things for others God has more than rewarded me. I read Oral Roberts's *Seed Faith* and no truer words were spoken: by giving yourself to others God rewards you doublefold."

ट&

"I think I have gone through a series of growth, regression, a little more growth, a slide, etc. With every step backward the need for prayer as an ongoing part of my whole day seems more apparent. I have never been one to read a series of written prayers constantly, but have always had my own special talks with God. I try to turn my daily routine household chores into a fun thing between Him and me. It has sustained me through a lot of boring jobs.

"I used to find the utmost peace and a closer communication with God in church. Now, I find I can communicate almost better within the confines of my own home. I don't think there is any 'best' way to pray. I do believe that the more one learns about the man Jesus and the harder one tries to pattern himself after Him, the closer one comes to knowing God intimately so that he can feel His presence always, rather than just when he is consciously working at it.

"Before my mother died, she said to me to pray as much as I could while I was able because 'as one grew old and sickly one just could not pray, although the presence of God was there.' A very dear friend of mine who happens to be a nun recently lost a Sister in her community who was in her early forties. This Sister told my friend to 'keep saying her office, no matter what, because if she ever couldn't she would realize even more the gift it is.' They say all truths are thrown before us as the hour of death draws near.

"To me, it all boils down to the same thing—God is one step closer with each prayer, regardless of what form that prayer takes, and He wants our prayers desperately."

ॐ

"I never really thought much about the way I pray, especially since lately it doesn't seem as though I do much praying, at least not in the oral sense. But I began to think, do I really pray, and if so, how? Oh, I had the typical training indigenous to a Catholic upbringing and there was a time when I tried to say the rosary every night. But over the past several years I've come to see that there can be a great difference between parroting words and actually communicating.

"I am not saying that I feel contempt for the traditional form of prayer. Any way that a person chooses to reach out to God is a beautiful thing and I respect the discipline that goes into saying the prayers one has learned. But for me the conventional way no longer seemed to have much meaning. I didn't feel as though I was reaching anything. I suppose this realization was one of the stepping-stones that led to my divorce: the awareness that there is a distinction between 'talking at' and 'communicating with,' that some people 'hear' but don't 'listen.'

"Communication is a truly intimate thing. It cannot be done without touching each other, at least mentally. I am a great believer in the natural order of things. If a person wants something to happen he should try to make it happen. If it is right for him, that is, natural, then under the proper conditions he should be able to achieve what he wants. If it is not right for him, if it would mean going against Nature's way to get it, then maybe he should reexamine his reasons for wanting it at all. Because if it is indeed against Nature then it can only hurt him in the long run. When we break the laws of Nature it is Life itself that punishes us. For that reason I've come to stop asking God *for* things. I know what I want, what I would like to have, and God knows too. But being human and with limited vision, I know that the things I want may at times not be good for me and that having them might be in violation of Nature. So, when Life does not afford me the things I would like,

I pray to our Lord for understanding and acceptance. Sometimes it takes a very strong faith to accept the fact that Nature's way, which is in fact God's way, is best for us, especially when we would have it otherwise.

"Maybe this faith in Nature is the reason I find I get so many answers to deep questions when I sit alone on a mountaintop or walk in solitude along the ocean shore. Without any distractions I view Nature, which is the umbilical cord between us and God, and as I meditate on things that are important to me I find the answers begin to unfold. I come to a realization of what the natural thing should be in certain situations. It is indeed God speaking to me and it makes me happy to feel He is so close. It's like two people who love each other or like a close loving relationship between parents and children, between brothers and sisters or between true friends. One becomes sensitive to the feelings of the other and many times words are not necessary. Thoughts are felt.

"I am always grateful for the answers I get. I try to show my thanks by living up to my new understanding (and that's not always easy). I guess what I'm trying to say is that to me prayer means action, but responsible action which comes as a result of a thoughtful search for guidance. And that guidance can only come from close communication with God.

"I still consider the saints to be my friends and at times I ask for their help. True friends don't always tell us exactly what we'd like to hear, but because they love us they want what's best for us. And since the saints see Truth more clearly than I do I appreciate the help of those special friends."

ह़े

"We've been taught all the facts in the Catholic Church, but what happened to me (who never fell away), I don't know. It all became hackneyed as the years went on. And I read and read and never stopped along the way. But, it was only last year when I began to make sacrifices in my life for certain people and joined a group of charismatics that I think I began to learn to pray.

"I could never carry a tune, but I learned to sing with these people. In singing—this may sound silly—I learned not only to raise my hands, but to close my eyes and exclude everyone else and concentrate on God. I heard Him speak to me, really, in a way I never had nor expected before. I am a very visual person. By this I mean I love and value my sight highly. Once, I was plunged into darkness (in a restaurant of all things) and I seemed to be without all my senses. I know that in church a great part of my experience has always been *looking* at other people and recognizing others that I knew, etc.

"Fortunately, I am also a sound oriented person. The effect of hearing the praying in tongues and the beautiful hymns that we sing (which are a great part of the service) and the glorious way in which they are sung has had a deep effect on me in bringing me closer to God.

"I feel very humble when I am with people who have been Pentecostals for fifty years and more and I realize that I have only recently been reborn. Yet, I probably have less than fifty years left to me.

"In February of 1973 the members of my Bible class gathered around me and laid their hands on, praying for my Baptism in the Spirit. I did none of the things that often accompany this. I walked home afterward and my gift was an amazing heightening of the visual—not blindingly so, like Paul on the road to Damascus, just an extreme brightness and clarity of everything that I looked at as I sang to myself all the way home. Then came a gradual unfolding of spiritual gifts that I could never have believed or comprehended if I had been told all that was to happen then. You can imagine how I look forward to the future!"

৯৯

"All my life I have prayed in some form: the simple prayers of childhood, the desperate prayers of fear and sorrow, the mechanical reciting of the daily rosary for thirty-four years. Ten to fifteen years ago I ventured into forms of meditation, or active contemplation. Since then, I can only say I believe God has led me along the path of pure contemplation, or mystical prayer. I say 'believe' because I feel that I am in the dark night spoken of by the Church Fathers, and yet I don't feel certain of anything. If this is true, and the indications make it appear so, I know I am only at the beginning of a long road.

"I feel God's presence continually; my love for Him is increasing; my faith and hope grow; my awareness of my sins intensifies without becoming overwhelming; my fear of and attachment to the world fades and I am starting to know what the words 'joy' and 'peace' mean. So as not to mislead, I wish to make clear that all these are directions rather than goals attained.

"The only prayer that I seem able to put into words is that God's will be done and that He will lead me to union with Him. That I may die completely to myself so that He can live in me as St. Paul experienced. Although I know Christ said we could pray for our needs, I find this difficult, as it seems that anything I ask for will be second-best to His will for me."

৯৯

This one is from a construction worker.

"I begin my day by rising at 5:45 A.M. I make the sign of the Cross, thank and praise the Lord for a new day and then bless my wife and each child, starting with the eldest, a fifteen-year old, down to the youngest, a two-year old. I have been blessed with nine beautiful children, and they aren't accidents. My wife and I love each one dearly. I am most grateful to God for all His blessings.

"I then go off to Mass. There is nothing more beautiful and greater than the Mass. It's my greatest strength. I grew up in poverty. My life has had many difficulties, but nothing has been so difficult that the Mass hasn't been my greatest source of strength. Before Mass, I spend a half-hour reading the Bible. I think about God's words.

"After a few moments of thanksgiving following Communion, I then go off to work thinking about the Lord's presence within me. I can't help but love the people I meet as I go on my way, for I know that God is with me. I bring His blessing with me. At the end of the Mass the priest gave me God's blessing. I ask God to extend that blessing to my wife, my children and everyone I meet.

"When I pray the 'Our Father' it takes me a long time to say it. I think about all that it means to me. My thoughts go something like this as I take each line:

"*Our Father,* our heavenly Father, Divine because you are God; beloved above all fathers because you gave us your only son to die on the cross for us; most devoted of all fathers, how great is your name. I say your name is great because so many use it wrongly.

"*Thy kingdom come,* the birth of your son who is our means of salvation. *Thy will be done on earth as it is in heaven.* This line makes me think of the Transfiguration of our Lord, when the Father said, 'This is my beloved Son; listen to Him.' I, in turn, listen to His words and accept all

His teachings and His will in my life; and I try to do all the good that I can.

"*Give us this day,* and throughout the days of our life and throughout all eternity, give us that Bread of Life of your Divine, blessed and most beloved son, Jesus—this Bread that feeds me spiritually and controls my humanity.

"Please, Father, *forgive us our trespasses* (I plead for my soul as for everyone) for which your Son has suffered. As we stand here before you, forgive our enemies who offend us. (When I look up at Christ hanging on the cross, I really can't have enemies, for I can't ask forgiveness for myself if I don't forgive my neighbor.) I'm no better than any other person on this earth. I'm grateful that I can even pray.

"*And deliver us from all evil,* guide us and protect us and always love us so that I may always love You through Your Divine Spirit. Amen."

ৡ৯

The following four reflections are from Roman Catholic Sisters.

"There are times when praying, for me, is *listening.* My most intense prayers have been 'said' in this manner. Before the Eucharistic presence, listening becomes a person-to-person conversation.

"When I have an opportunity to be outdoors, the beauty of nature, in whatever form it might be—clouds, trees, earth—makes me conscious of the God above and His loving concern for me. I find myself *talking* to Him in a sense of gratitude, e.g., 'Lord, you have made this just for me. I love it. One would have been enough, but you don't do things in a small way, your love is limitless. Please give me more of it?'

"I have prayer books, too, from which I *read* my prayers. This form of prayer gives a certain type of discipline to my life, from which I enjoy inner peace."

కఴ

"When I awaken in the early morning, my eyes meet the distant, beautiful horizon of a new, bright, love-filled day. I bounce out of bed as if from a springboard. I'm filled with joy, thrilled at the prospect of a grace-laden day. God you're great!

"I am ready in no time and out on the walk, loving God, praising, thanking, praying to Him among trees, birds, sky. I unite with all who are praying. God you're great! I want to lift up my hands to you, but people might think I've gone out of my mind. I have! My heart is filling, my heart is happy. God, you are so good. My Father, my Creator, this is only a taste of your love.

"In this union, I prepare myself for the Eucharistic liturgy which begins in a half-hour. Then I enter the chapel and begin the solemn communion with Him, and through Him and in Him. Great God, how wonderful you are! One day, I will live with You and forever enjoy the eternal day, which eye has not seen, nor ears heard, nor has it entered into the heart of man to conceive. I believe. My God, I love you.

"At night I again enter the chapel, sit on a cushion, my head against the wall, relaxed, quiet, reinforcing my values, emptying myself, going deeper, canceling out negative thoughts. Alone with God—*my* God."

కఴ

"Living in His presence requires no images, no symbols, no words. Rather, it is a 'tasting and a seeing' which opens us to another dimension of life. The world and His people are perceived through His eyes. His Spirit fills me with understanding, silent and tranquil, and He awakens in me a 'hunger and thirst' for truth and mercy. Praise, thanksgiving, surrender, flow from His grace-filled 'touch.' (To experience is to understand.)

"God is *Love*, and love is other-centered, life-giving. I have felt urged to share in His redemptive prayer to the Father who seeks to heal humanity of the pain of its incompleteness. In part, it means shouldering my own cross joyfully and willingly, bearing it as He did His for others.

"Sometimes for long periods—years, a decade—prayer has been darkness and search, longing and the sense of abandonment. At these moments, faith has struggled to assure me, not always too successfully, that even this, offered 'through Him, with Him and in Him,' can help to bring to fulfillment all that He creates, redeems and sanctifies."

ತಾ

"All that I can offer God now is myself, my tiny bit of physical work and pain, plus the longing to continue to be of use to all. Please understand, I am an old lady trying to be ever closer and closer to my Divine Spouse and yet, and here is the paradox, very worldly in thoughts and acts.

"How do I pray? A very salutary question. At one time I thought I was praying only when I was able to kneel before our Lord in the Blessed Sacrament. Then came the realization that teaching was prayer. Our Order's wise rules made the balance between prayers on knees and prayers at work. But now there is dryness, aridity and very seldom 'sweetness.' It is my own fault, but all that I can manage is 'Praise Jesus!' or 'Come, O Holy Spirit'—a few ejaculations and trying to find Him in the Sisters and older people here."

ह๑

These are all beautiful accounts of personal experiences of prayer. As you can see, they are at slightly different levels in their development. Some are freer than others from self-doubt and guilt, but each reveals the inner heart of a person who is in love with God. All of them show clearly the spirit of gratitude beneath the emotions of their present state of life.

It is not for us to judge anyone's prayer. All prayer is beautiful and we can gain some perspective on our own prayer life by observing others. We are, after all, only human. All it takes is a sensible effort to communicate with God.

Contemplation, or the enjoyment of God, requires no words. Many of the contributors to this chapter have enjoyed God but they do not know how to put it into words because the experience is indescribable. All of us have the same goal, namely, to honor God by believing in His love and His union with us, and by enjoying Him.

CHAPTER V

Learning to Trust the Lord

How much we depend on our own powers; how little we depend on God. And yet God is everything; without Him we are nothing.

Saint Paul says, "We see now through a glass darkly." We muddle along with our imperfect understanding of reality. Our grasp of knowledge is shaded and discolored because our minds need light to illuminate what is before us. The Lord gives us knowledge of His mysteries at a pace suited to our receptive powers. Jesus has told us: "Seek and you shall find. Ask and you shall receive." And this is true. So, to receive more, we are invited to desire more. The way God responds to our desire has a name: actual grace. A particular type of actual grace is described by Saint Thomas as *Lumen Intellectus,* light to the mind. There are moments when we are given a flash of insight. In a moment of revelation we see things in a new way. We may have thought we knew them already, but with actual grace a veil is lifted from our eyes.

For Jesus, the Father was everything. He was the center of His life. His whole purpose, motivation and activity was directed to Him. He had come to do His Father's will. Jesus was a *man for others* only in the sense that the Father sent Him to save mankind. He was more a *man for the Father.* He allowed the Father to lead Him. Because we know this, we often try to imitate Jesus. We too want to find out what the Father's will is for us. We look for it as though it was a *thing* out there, something to be found, the way one finds a lost key. Some of us decide what we want and then convince ourselves it is what God wants for us. Others discern what God wants in more or less general terms and then work feverishly to do what is expected.

Religion can deteriorate into a struggle to demonstrate (primarily to oneself) one's constancy, one's integrity, one's thoughtfulness, one's willingness to serve, one's piety. It becomes "I must do this"; "I will do that"; "I must not do the other thing." Please notice the use of the word "I"— I, I, I. Religion becomes self-centered. This is why good people become ashamed when they see their own weakness and disheartened when they fail to improve. They have not yet learned "abandonment." They have tried to do *too much on their own.*

In his book *He Leadeth Me,* Father Walter Ciszek, a Jesuit who was a prisoner in Russia for twenty-three years, put his moment of truth in these words:

> Slowly, reluctantly, under the gentle proddings of grace,
> I faced the truth that was at the root of my problem
> and my shame. The answer was a single word: *I.*
> I was ashamed because I knew in my heart I had tried to
> do too much and I had failed. I felt guilty because
> I realized, finally, that I had asked for God's help but
> had really believed in my own ability to avoid evil and to
> meet every challenge. I had spent much time in prayer
> over the years. I had come to appreciate and thank God
> for His Providence and care of me and of all men,
> but I never really abandoned myself to it. . . . In short,
> I felt guilty and ashamed because in the last analysis
> I had relied almost completely on myself in this most
> critical test—and I had failed.*

* Walter Ciszek, S.J., *He Leadeth Me* (New York: Doubleday and Co., 1973), pp. 73, 74.

Until we learn the truth of our total dependence on Him, we will not be free from the tyranny of self.

Someone once compared the soul to a glass. In order for it to be filled with life-sustaining water, it must first be clean and empty. The soul too must be emptied of self for the Lord to fill it with His precious gifts. But these are words. The truth of the matter is that I am learning about it myself. Little by little, I see it more clearly and even hold it for a day or so, this feeling of being in the Lord, totally His, acting out of a knowledge that He is indeed leading me, but then it goes away. The mad pace, the constant phone calls and visits, the streams of activity that flood each day: all of these seem to make total abandonment an impossibility. Even when these preoccupations are what might be called God's work, they still pull me apart, leaving me tired, dazed and at times feeling as though God was far away indeed. I know better, but I feel it just the same. Feelings can so often distort reality. I wondered how my friend Father Ciszek handled it in his own life. So I asked him about it one day.

"How does it work?" I asked him. "I mean abandoning yourself to God—what do you do when you find it impossible to be really abandoned?" (Remember, Father Ciszek had spent twenty-three years at hard labor and in solitary confinement in Moscow and Siberian prisons.) I took notes as he spoke in his quiet, rapid way. This is what he said:

> When I first discovered the importance of abandonment, I didn't know whether I was making any progress or not. When I tried to move more deeply into a state of abandonment, I had the feeling that I was not doing it right, that this was not it. So I'd ask the Lord, "What do I do?" "How do I do it?" You don't make much progress at first because you keep coming back to self; but you know you're in a new area. You aren't affected as

much by your own failure or unsuccess as you used to be. You grow away from some of the ideas you had about proving yourself, about human courage, and things like that.

What you were before isn't eliminated—it keeps coming back—but a steady growing takes place, a new consciousness of God's control over you, a new attitude toward things as they happen. Temptations don't hit you quite the same way. You learn grace isn't only in the good things, but in the bad things as well. The misuse of grace is the mistake we make. We forget that God brings good out of everything.

You begin to realize that whether you succeed or not is God's business. You get a freer perspective on your life. God is teaching you all the time about what you are and what you are not, to help you really live the life of abandonment. He leads you more deeply into the atmosphere of abandonment. You learn that what you do or do not do in your spiritual program doesn't matter so much; what matters is the spirit in which you are working at the time. I see God in me asking me to say Mass. You have to be convinced in faith that God is asking you to do it. This gives you trust, and if everything else fails, trust will save you.

Trust is the key word. I began to see more clearly that it is at the basis of true dependence on the Lord. Father Ciszek closed his remarks with this rather strange image:

My role is that of a sunken bucket. . . . It's on the bottom, deep, no movement, no bubbles. I sink myself into God like that; He has complete access to me. He is the One that moves me; He does everything; I do nothing.

But how? How does one achieve the state of total

dependence on God? The answer is simple: one doesn't achieve it at all; one receives it. It is not something acquired, like the skill of typing or the art of playing the piano. It is a gift from God; no one can give it to himself. We fail to depend on God whenever we depend too much on ourselves—our own ability, our own strength, our own determination. The realization of our utter dependence on God dawns on us only imperceptibly over a long period of time; it is a gift that God Himself reveals ever so slowly. All we can do is desire it and pray for the grace to grow less self-reliant and more and more dependent on the Lord.

Perhaps we can do a little more. We can begin by examining our lives thoughtfully to see if we have fallen into any of the traps that the ego sets for us. For instance, it is an all too human fault to make believe the Father's will for us coincides with our own desires. The more we want something, i.e., the more we depend on it for our happiness, the more we tend to assume that it is surely what God must also want. When this happens we may not be listening; we may be dictating.

When we see one solution, one goal for our life, we usually presume that God approves it and will therefore help us to reach it. If He doesn't, we are baffled. We learn soon enough that man's ways are not God's ways. We underestimate the role of pride. Many things that we do, not only our daily work, but even our ascetical practices, are not done solely in response to God's grace, but out of pride. This is a key point. We are not always attuned to the inspiration of the Holy Spirit; it takes a listening heart; it takes discernment. A spiritual director, or confessor, may be of help here. Confession is not merely for sinners; it is a sacrament which brings the grace of discernment. We need reassurance that we are on the right track. The challenge is not so much one of doing good and avoiding evil; it is one of allowing the Lord to lead us so that we do only that good which He assigns. Remember, doing *too much on our own* is a great danger. Some good must be left for others to do. We can only do some good and avoid some evil.

Pride has many insidious ways of trapping us. The more we trust in our own powers, the less we depend on God. We were created to do His will in all things. Our own intellect and willpower can carry us only so far. When we fail we become disheartened because we allowed ourselves to believe that it is in our power to become holy. It is not. God is teaching us over and over again that it is He who is purifying us, not we ourselves. He does this in His own way, at His own pace. When we run ahead of Him he leaves us on our own and we usually stumble. When He leaves us to depend on our own strength, we soon learn that there is little strength in us. We may suffer one humiliation after another, until it begins to dawn on us that He is everything. We either gradually learn to trust Him or we continue to trust ourselves.

Let me give you an example of an extraordinary trusting spirit in our own time. Mother Teresa of Calcutta, with her community of sisters, serves the poorest of the poor all over the world. She turned down a gift of $500,000 because it had strings attached. The donor wanted the money invested and the interest each year to go to the sisters to make their lives more secure in the future. Mother Teresa said that since the poor whom they serve have no security, and do not know where their next meal is coming from, the sisters should be no different. Their vow of poverty requires that they, too, renounce the kind of security the world of money gives. She accepts gifts for her work, but not with an eye to improving the lot of the sisters. Alms are taken only to be used in the service of the poor and for the day-to-day maintenance of the sisters.

What foolishness, you say? Couldn't that money be used for the sisters anyway with the extra income applied to the poor? Interest on $500,000 is more than $25,000 a year. With a windfall like that Mother Teresa could have advanced her community in many ways, but she was acting out of a higher wisdom. That kind of holiness appears to be folly even to good men and women.

Once, I heard of a community of sisters who were working with the very poor. I went to see what I could do for them in my spare time. I was amazed at their poverty. Their religious habits were worn and patched; their shoes were bursting at the seams; their food seemed to be the mere subsistence level—beans, rice, milk—with rarely any meat or fish. They were in the middle of one of the poorest sections of the city and the people loved them, especially the children. Meeting these sisters awakened in me a great desire for holiness. I worked for them, helping them in any way I could, and I was overjoyed to be among such a happy community of holy women.

Years later, I returned to the same community to visit my old friends. The sisters did not seem the same. A beautiful new convent had been built with money donated by a wealthy benefactor. The table was filled with choice food; a huge fence surrounded the compound and the neighborhood children were no longer free to enter the convent grounds. I also detected a quality of sadness among many of the remaining sisters. When I spoke out about what I saw the warm welcome I had been given was replaced by fear, suspicion, distrust and, on the part of some, rejection. The sisters deserved the very best—I don't deny that—but something powerful went out of that community when they decided to move away from their former spirit of poverty. Mother Teresa's trust was not in money, but in God. This is the radical kind of dependence on God that inspires others. Holiness isn't easily understood. Christ's wisdom is not perceived or accepted by everyone, but it is superior to human wisdom.

Trust is the love answer. Trust is more enjoyable than worry. It often happens that our nerves upset us and cause us to feel insecure. Our faith at times seems to falter. All of this happens when we fail to trust the Lord. There are many who turn their life over to Christ and try to abandon themselves to God's will. Yet, after a while, they begin to feel that the Lord never heard them, that they are in fact left dangling in the same old way. They feel abandoned *by* Him, rather than abandoned *to* Him. They feel distress, discomfort, confusion, doubt and alienation. All of us at times may have felt this way. The strange thing is that we tend to believe these feelings when they come, even though we know better. Saint Francis de Sales once said: "Do not be discouraged because you are discouraged." What a wise man he was. That idea can be expanded. Do not be nervous because you are nervous; do not be anxious because you are anxious. Moods and emotions are passing things. It's normal to be nervous and upset at times. It is not a moral problem or a spiritual danger sign, just part of the human condition. Out of failure, pain and sorrow can come great progress. All growth is painful. Remember, just because you feel abandoned does not mean that God has really abandoned you. So do not overreact to your own sense of failure.

Many people are afraid when there is absolutely nothing to fear. Some little children are afraid of a bogeyman in the closet; but there is no bogeyman in the closet. Some grown-ups are terrified in elevators or when they look out of a tenth-story window, but there is no objective danger. False feeilngs exaggerate and distort reality. Feelings do not teach us facts, but faith does. Reading Scripture sometimes helps when we are anxious. Here is a remarkable passage that may be of help:

> We are quite confident that if we ask for anything and it is in accordance with His will, He will hear us; and knowing that whatever we may ask, He is listening, we know that we have already been granted what we asked of Him (I John 5:14-15).

Since you have already told God you need Him and have asked for His help, you know He hears you in spite of the fact that you may feel He doesn't. We have to learn the technique of overcoming fear and doubt. There are many ways to protect yourself from your emotions. Why not guard yourself against discouragement and disbelief by creating your own wall of defense against those feelings that distort the facts taught to you by faith? Believe only one thing: that you can put your trust in Jesus Christ, true God and true Man. Jesus is your Lord. He is your protector. You can depend on His love and power. It is very easy to pray, but if you really believe in Him and want to please Him, you must trust. Trust is the love answer.

Only God sees the whole picture. Each life is filled with shadow and light. Jesus Christ knew this. He experienced what it means to be human. Good Friday and Easter Sunday are the poles of shadow and light in His life.

The great paintings of Rembrandt are characterized by the artist's genius in capturing the play of light. His figures seem to emerge from darkness into a cascade of golden brilliance. But to attain this effect, Rembrandt had to spend considerable time mixing dark colors to create the shadows. If you had come upon him working at those times, you might have thought he was trying to produce a sad and gloomy work. But, no. With a little patience you would realize that the dark colors show off the golden light in its best setting.

The Lord of life is a great artist and we are His creation. Each of us is a work in progress, a masterpiece in the making. There are times in our life when we are lost in the shadows, when moods are dark, when the world seems hostile, when our best efforts fail, when we become full of fear and doubt. We feel as though the light has gone out of us because we do not see the whole picture. But things are never as bleak as they seem. We so easily misread the signs, see only the shadows and miss the glorious reality of the finished product.

To be redeemed in the Blood of Christ and to be offered the promise of eternal life is part of the total Christian experience of human existence. Why, then, are we not joyful in our daily life? Instead of singing with joy and thanksgiving, we often become discouraged and seem to assume a posture of resignation. We think the worst, and this is a distortion of the truth. Only God has the whole picture and only faith can lift us out of our own dark interpretation of human events.

Life is a splendid, glorious adventure. The shadows are there and they have their purpose. Because of them we are more ready to treasure the rays of golden sunshine. They must be seen in context. The Resurrection of Jesus was preceded by pain. As terrible as that pain was, it was a saving pain; it was the coin that purchased our redemption. God does draw good from evil and we need only trust that He will do the same in our lives.

The Master is at work in each life. He writes straight with crooked lines. He is bringing us to glory and happiness.

The dominant theme of life is hopeful, full of promise, and for this we are grateful. Can we trust Him? Can we believe this truth with all the power and strength of our being? It is more than something we know. It is something we must *decide*. Faith requires more than mere intellectual assent. It requires decision—the will to accept Jesus Christ as loving Savior. We reject anything and everything that will undermine our confidence in Him. To love Him is to thank Him "always and everywhere."

Abandonment to God leads to sweetness of spirit. Abandonment to Almighty God involves a high level of trust in the Lord. We have to pray for the grace to grow in this insight. But do not be discouraged because you are not able to achieve the ideal of "total abandonment." There is an infallible way to measure your spiritual state. It has nothing to do with fancy concepts; it has to do with sweetness of spirit.

Where charity is, there God is. By their fruits you will know them. A person may not be consciously abandoned to God. Nevertheless, he may exude a sweetness of spirit that is a blessing in itself for all those around him. This is not so say that the person is a sentimental pushover, incapable of getting angry when there is justification. It means that he is fundamentally forgiving, gentle, open and willing to be of help wherever possible. Christians and non-Christians whose lives have been touched by God in a beautiful way are capable of possessing a loving heart. The Holy Spirit breathes where He will. Sweetness of spirit is not our exclusive property. It can be found among Jews, Moslems, Buddhists, Hindus and others.

On the other hand, there are many Christians who are wounded and hurt. Instead of turning the hurt to the Lord, they allow themselves to become sour. There are some obvious danger signs: a spirit of negativism or vituperation and an ever present display of self-righteousness. This is not the moral indignation of the prophet but the bitterness of the self-pitying complainer. Not only individuals, but whole familities and groups can be infected with a bitter spirit. It is often justified in the name of religion. When this happens, it is obvious that something has gone awry. Although there are serious problems in life which leave people angry or grief-stricken, the Christian should come back to that sweetness of spirit that characterizes charity. When a person is always sour it means trouble. The sour spirit is not from God. He calls us to be grateful in all circumstances.

A prayer written by a prisoner was found in a Nazi concentration camp. It asked God to look mercifully upon the prison guards; to remember not the cruelty and pain they inflicted, but rather the great virtues of patience, love and fraternal loyalty that their actions evoked from the prisoners, one toward the other. How sweet was the spirit that conceived such a prayer.

When dying on the cross, Christ, who is the model of sweetness, said: "Forgive them Father, for they know not what they do." This is the spirit He has put in us. We stand firm in the power of His Name. Abandonment surely will lead to this fragrant flower of humility and love. But for those who are not comfortable with the idea of self-abandonment as an attainable goal, there is still reason to be peaceful and hopeful. God's ways are mysterious. He brings forth good fruit where He will, in season and out. He draws good out of everything, if we ask. We all stand in His power; we all benefit from His love. All we need know is that a decision must be made by each one of us. That decision, the decision as to the kind of a person we are going to be, sweet or sour, is entirely our own. We are in great need of help, especially when everything seems to justify the sour, bitter spirit in us. *Where love is, there God is.*

The Lord has asked us to trust Him with so great a trust that our lives would then no longer be recognizable as our own. He asks us to live one day at a time. If we do, we no longer will be anxious about tomorrow nor about all the tomorrows of our life, the future state of our health, our financial position, our loved ones. I am not saying that we will be spaced out, unconcerned about our responsibilities. We will, however, be free from the hours of needless worry that darken our lives. If we can free ourselves, if we can attain such a plateau, we will be utterly different. We will be free because we will surely believe that the future is in God's hands. All we need to do is to make a sensible effort, a reasonable effort, and He will do the rest. If we do, we will learn to live for today.

Is this so absurd and unattainable? I wonder. Consider the Alcoholics Anonymous program and the widespread success it has achieved in transforming lives. It works. It works because it follows the natural law. The alcoholic is in a hopeless state, totally dependent on his addiction, irresponsible, inconsiderate, insensitive toward others. His future can only be one of desolation and pain. His guilt over past sins and cruelties crushes his self-respect and offers little hope for a redeemed life. Can there be a future for him?

AA offers a simple spiritual program which comes right out of the gospel of Jesus Christ, though the members need not be Christian to benefit from it. Once the alcoholic realizes he has hit bottom, AA provides two strong pillars on which he can build his personal renewal: (1) He can learn to depend not on himself, but on the Supreme Being, however he may conceive Him. (2) He can learn to live life one day at a time.

An AA member only has to get through one twenty-four hour period. He has to make it till bedtime without taking a drink. This principle can be applied to any addiction, any sinful need. It is easier to live today when we block out the things required of us in the future. Christ's words "Sufficient unto the day" have special significance for us because, in learning to block out the problems of tomorrow, we are at the same time cognizant of the fact that they must be faced sooner or later. In the meantime, we entrust them to God. We take confidence from the fact that they are *His* problems now and that we need only to concern ourselves with getting through one day at a time, without sin, without neglecting our spiritual needs.

If an alcoholic can muster enough strength from God to transform ugliness into sweetness—and we know he can because hundreds of thousands have done so—then, you, with your many blessings and gifts, can add immeasurable sweetness to your spirit by living life one day at a time. The future is in God's hands. You need only draw upon His strength to carry you through this day.

By living just for today we block out worries about the future. Most things we worry about never come to pass and the things that hurt us the most are usually beyond our control anyway. Thank God we can't see into the future. If we could we probably would become paralyzed with fear. We are not meant to see the future except insofar as to know that the mercy, goodness and the Providence of God will prevail over all evil.

To live each day fully is to be present in the *now* of time. So many people are haunted by their past mistakes. The suffering of the present is directly related to what they believe to be some past error. It hardly ever occurs to them that the mistake might be providential and that God's glory will be manifest in His forgiveness and healing. The painful syndrome repeats itself: "If only I had it to live over again."

The present day can be ruined by feelings of guilt and anguish. Today can be eaten up with resentment and contempt over injustices suffered at the hands of another. It can be ruined by suppressed anger over not having been loved well enough in the past. *But today is all we have.* If we are ever to be happy and at peace it will be in the now of our life, not tomorrow. We can unconsciously ruin today by carrying the weight of all our yesterdays and all our tomorrows in the here and now. That's too much for anyone. Christ told us not to be anxious. He assured us of His healing and forgiveness. He promised us anything if we ask the Father in His Name. So why do we labor needlessly with these obsessions from the past which only serve to stir up our passions and rob us of much needed peace? Why do we not ask for the power to accept forgiveness and be done with it?

The past is over. It is done with, no more. It no longer can touch us or hurt us or penetrate our deepest being— not even if we have present crosses that relate to past mistakes. Christ gave us the wisdom to understand what we must do: "Take up your cross and follow me." "Sufficient unto the day are the day's troubles." Even though all our instincts direct us to throw off the cross and construct our own future, Christ says, "Take up your cross."

These words have been spoken and written so often that they seem repetitious and unnecessary. We are, however, much in need of returning again and again to the fountain of wisdom, in need to be reminded of the simple truths of our faith, to realize we must live one day at a time and accept healing and forgiveness for past errors with songs of gladness. (The knowledge of forgiveness is a great joy.) It is an act of trust to detach ourselves from needless worry—an act thoroughly pleasing to the Lord. *Trust is the love answer.*

CHAPTER VI

Practicing the Presence of God

At times each of us needs to try something a little different in our approach to prayer. Prayer is not so much a matter of mastering one technique and persevering with it for the rest of your life. You can see how impossible that would be, humanly speaking; rather, it is an internal effort to communicate with God. This "touching of spirits" will take many different forms in your life. One approach worth cultivating is to practice the presence of God.

My former spiritual director for more than twenty years was Father James McCoy, S.J. He was called to God in 1977 at the age of seventy-seven. He used to find long meditation difficult and so he would direct his mind and heart to God by using short ejaculations in which he praised God, thanked Him or asked Him for some particular grace. In terms of loving Jesus, he was devoted to the Eucharist. He went directly to the Divine Lord present in the sacrament of the Eucharist.

"Eucharistic Jesus, I need and I want efficacious grace to know Thee, to love Thee and to serve Thee." He repeated this over and over again throughout the day.

An efficacious grace is a grace that is one-hundred

percent effective. Not every actual grace given by God is accepted or cooperated with properly. This grace is a light to the intellect or an impulse to the will which effectively accomplishes its purpose. My friend Father James explained the words of the prayer to me: "I need," because I am a creature and my life is a perilous journey. "I want," because it is my supreme desire to grow in His love. "I want efficacious grace," because without His gifts I can do nothing, see nothing, love nothing. "To know Thee," because when somebody hurts or offends me I want to turn my mind to Him. "To love Thee," because it is my destiny to love Him. "To serve Thee," because I want to serve myself less and yield more to His Holy Will.

There are many approaches to praying short ejaculations. The above approach is obviously only one of them.

The Jesus Prayer is another approach that has recently become very popular. The need for this type of brief prayer has become increasingly apparent in the lives of busy people because a long, sustained period of prayer is for them next to impossible. As a result they tend to neglect their prayer life altogether. You must take nourishment for a healthy body. Prayer in any form is spiritual nourishment.

The Jesus Prayer, "Lord Jesus Christ, have mercy on me," is used repeatedly throughout the day. It is an ancient practice of the Russian Christians. When a person recites these words frequently in the firm belief that *Jesus' presence is within them, that His very presence brings holiness and that their own unworthiness counts for nothing,* a transformation of spirit takes place. Even though the words are mumbled over and over again, it is not a matter of merely mouthing pious phrases. It is a question of taking nourishment from God, enjoying His love. The prayer reminds you that Jesus is in you and that He makes you holy by His power and presence. If you can keep to this idea you will progress rapidly.

Time for quiet prayer will come about naturally, no longer fixed by schedules and willpower; meditation will become easier and more frequent because the will to unite with Jesus is constant. You may never actually succeed in consciously praying all the time—and maybe that is not important anyway—but the very desire to pray always, the will to pray always, sets up a new life tempo. It not only makes you aware of God's presence but also protects you from becoming discouraged. The art is not in concentrating on the words, but in enjoying God's continual love.

In Luke 18:1-8 we find: "Jesus told them this parable to teach them that they should always pray and never become discouraged. There was a judge in a certain town who neither feared God nor respected men. And there was a widow in that same town who kept coming to him and pleading for her rights: 'Help me against my opponent!' For a long time the judge was not willing, but at last he said to himself, 'Even though I don't fear God or respect men, yet because of all the trouble this widow is giving me, I will see to it that she gets her rights, or else she will keep on coming and finally wear me out!' And the Lord continued: 'Listen to what that corrupt judge said. Now, will God not judge in favor of his own people who cry to him for help day and night? Will he be slow to help them? I tell you, he will judge in their favor, and do it quickly. But will the Son of Man find faith on earth when he comes?' "

Here we see Jesus encouraging us to be constant in prayer and to have faith that God is listening. There are many housewives, office workers, people in all walks of life, who have never thought of themselves as prayerful but for years have repeated short ejaculations to suit their

needs. They have developed a simple direct line to God
and many of them actually live constantly in His presence.
They may not feel very worthy, or very spiritual, but that
is not for them to judge. Humility is a good sign. It is one
of the indications of holiness and, since God shields us
from vainglory through the pains and troubles of our life,
it is not farfetched to say that the saints are the first ones
to disclaim their holiness.

In the parable, Christ exhorts us to imitate the per-
sistent widow who, even though dealing with a corrupt and
selfish judge, finally won her hearing. The key to her
character was the fact that she really wanted something.
The key to our negligence in prayer is that we really do
not hunger and thirst after holiness. Faith has a way of
putting first things first. Even if you do not fully understand
what is being said here, pray for mercy, healing and holiness, and pray with persistence. "Lord Jesus Christ have
mercy on me."

Permit me to share with you a little of my own experience with the Jesus Prayer. As far back as I can remember,
I always wanted to improve and deepen my prayer life.
I never felt that I was succeeding. There were a lot of
years, when I was growing up, when I hardly prayed at
all and there were some years—in the seminary especially—
when I prayed perhaps too intensely. But all the while I
experienced a sense of dissatisfaction: I should pray more;
I should pray better. One particular concern of mine was
with the First Epistle of Paul to the Thessalonians where we
are admonished to "pray without ceasing."

How can anyone pray constantly? It's impossible, I
thought. We have so many cares and concerns that plague
us during the day; they even invade our guarded moments
of solitude when we try to speak to God. One cannot go
off to a contemplative monastery, which seems to be the

only place where constant prayer might be plausible (but I'm told by monks and nuns who have worked at it for years that the monastery is not as still and silent as it is cracked up to be). How, then, can one take seriously something as demanding as Paul's exhortation?

One of the ways I found to help me approach this ideal—which I have never attained perfectly—an ideal that makes sense to me, is the Jesus Prayer. It may not work for you, and if so then let it be, but I offer it anyway, just in case. The first time I came across the idea was in J. D. Salinger's book *Franny and Zooey* quite a few years ago. The main character is a mixed-up young man who is searching for answers to life's big questions. He discovers the Jesus Prayer by reading an old Russian book called *The Way of a Pilgrim* and gets all enthused with it. He learns that the ancient Eastern Fathers of the Church had taught about this form of prayer. Naturally, I was interested myself and made a mental note to read *The Way of a Pilgrim* someday. But I couldn't find a copy and eventually it all passed from memory until a few years later when a friend recommended that I look into and begin the practice of the Jesus Prayer. I was surprised to have this idea reawakened and I agreed to it, but the desire only lasted about two weeks.

This is an example of how actual grace works. We sometimes get the light to the mind by way of a preparation for something else; the impulse to the will does not come until later. In my case "the later" was a few years later, when I stumbled upon a translation of the old Russian manual *The Way of a Pilgrim* (Seabury Press) by accident in a bookstore. I found it an extremely helpful and interesting exercise.

What is the Jesus Prayer? Let the unknown Russian author explain it to you directly. It might be better called

"The Continual Practice of the Presence of Jesus," instead
of the Jesus Prayer: "The continuous interior Prayer of
Jesus is a constant uninterrupted calling upon the Divine
Name of Jesus . . . in the spirit, in the heart, *while forming
a mental picture of His constant presence,* and imploring
His grace during every occupation, at all times, in all places,
even during sleep. The appeal (or prayer) is put in these
terms, 'Lord Jesus Christ, have mercy on me.' " He continues: "One who accustoms himself to this appeal experiences as a result so deep a consolation and so great a need
to offer the prayer always, that he can no longer live without it and it will continue to voice itself within him of its
own accord."

It's not easy to form such a habit. In fact, it's practical-
ly impossible. Perseverance is needed; it is surprising how
the prayer pops back in your mind after you've forgotten it.
The petition need not always be "have mercy on me," for
even as we think of others, loved ones and friends, we recite
the prayer for them as well. "Lord Jesus Christ have mercy
on them." When Saint Paul said "Pray without ceasing,"
the early Eastern Fathers believed he meant just that.

There are some who think of prayer exclusively as the
rare moment of deep communion with God, as though the
day was made up of profane time and sacred time. This is
inaccurate. Prayer makes time sacred; continual prayer
makes all time sacred. The Jesus Prayer can serve as a
prelude to contemplation, but it is not merely a means to
something better. It is gospel-inspired, authentic prayer.
The Jesus Prayer has converted alcoholics and prostitutes;
it has strengthened priests and contemplatives. It sets up a
basic predisposition in the spirit, a condition of surrender to
a power greater than self, the power of Almighty God.
Through surrender to Christ we are made children of the
Father, acknowledging our true place in the universe. This,

for the sinner, is a reckless conversion of heart, a frame of mind that secures the soul in peace and freedom from the demon that controls and destroys.

Doubters will ask, is it really praying if we merely repeat the same words over and over? Even Jesus told us not to multiply words. But, as I mentioned earlier, it is not merely the words that are involved. It is the practice of the Presence of Jesus Christ in a spirit of joy that is the heart of this prayer.

In the gospel of Saint Mark (14:32-40), we read of how Christ, in the Agony of the Garden, is filled with sorrow to the point of death. "He kept saying, 'Abba (O Father) you have the power to do all things. Take this cup from me. But let it be as you would have it, not as I.'" Notice how He repeats a theme of the Lord's Prayer, "Thy will be done," only here in different words. He goes to Peter and finds him asleep and says, "Be on guard and pray that you may not be put to the test." He wants Peter to be more constant in prayer. In that urging, we too are reminded of the great themes of Christianity. We need prayer always, almost as background music to our work, our conversation, our daily round of activities. In the Gospel account, Jesus returned after speaking with Peter and repeated the same thought: "Going back again He began to pray in the same words." It is Christ's example that urges us to constant prayer.

There are moments of trial and temptation, happiness and thanksgiving, anxiety and petition, awe and devotion, sorrow and repentance, when the Jesus Prayer can fill your heart with sweetness and peace. You call upon Jesus always and everywhere to express your awareness of His loving presence. "Lord Jesus Christ have mercy on me."

Maybe you do not pray enough. Why not try to correct the situation. Not by resolving to pray each morning, but to pray always. As Christ said to the sleeping Peter, "Rouse yourself and come along" (Mark 14:42). It doesn't matter if your head swims with worry over petty things or if your state of life is not as admirable as it should be. To begin, you only need to say the words, draw closer to Christ. The one who knocks constantly will be heard. Jesus has promised it.

How do you actually begin to pray? It isn't difficult. Study the gospel for direction. First, turn to Matthew 6:5-8:

> When you are praying do not behave like hypocrites who love to stand and pray in Churches [synagogues] or on street corners in order to be noticed. Whenever you go to your room, close the door, and pray to your Father in private. Then your Father, who sees what no man sees, will repay you. In your prayer do not rattle on like the pagans. They think they will win a hearing by the sheer multiplication of words. Do not imitate them. Your Father knows what you need before you ask Him.

There are a couple of themes in this passage that might discourage someone in the use of the Jesus Prayer. Let's deal with them directly. First, we know that private prayer should have the worship of God as its primary purpose. To pray in order to be known as a prayerful person or for any reason other than to ask for forgiveness, to adore God, to thank God or to seek His favor is to misunderstand the whole meaning of worship. In saying the words of the Jesus Prayer, "Lord Jesus Christ have mercy on me," over and over again, we are acknowledging Jesus as Lord and we are pleading for His healing love. Repeating the same words is the way Christ taught us to pray. It is a good and holy thing as long as we inform the words with the proper spirit. In warning us not to rattle on like the pagans, Jesus is condemning the mindless, heartless prayer-wheel mentality, not the repetition of the practice of the Divine Presence which is also a call for Divine help and grace.

Remember, also, that Christ laid down a condition in order for our prayer to be effective: "If you forgive the faults of others, your heavenly Father will forgive you yours. If you do not forgive others, neither will your Father forgive you" (Matt. 6:14-15). These words must be taken seriously. We all tend to grumble and complain too much. We need to practice positive charity more than we do. It is rare when a person is being criticized to hear someone else speak up in his or her defense, not merely forgiving them, but reminding others of their good qualities. Shouldn't we all try to be more understanding, more forgiving? The effectiveness of our own prayer depends on it.

If you read further in Matthew (7:7-12), you will learn how to succeed in prayer, how to be bold in hope and deep in union with God: "Ask and you will receive. Seek and you will find. Knock and it will be opened to you. For the one who asks, receives. The one who seeks, finds. The one who knocks, enters. Would one of you hand his son a stone when he asks for a loaf, or a poisonous snake when he asks for a fish? If you with all your sins know how to give your children what is good, how much more will your heavenly Father give good things to anyone who asks Him!"

To enjoy God you have to understand the power of this love. The Jesus Prayer is one way to be present to God's unchanging love. It is not necessary to use these exact words. Any formula of words to bring to mind the presence of love will do as well. Acts of faith, hope and love are excellent substitutes. More important than the words themselves is the spirit of joy which the presence of God evokes in the heart. Enjoy the Lord.

For the desire of your heart is itself your prayer. And if
the desire is constant, so is your prayer. The Apostle Paul
had a purpose in saying: 'Pray without ceasing.' Are we
then ceaselessly to bend our knees, to lie prostrate, or
to lift up our hands? Is this what is meant in saying: 'Pray
without ceasing?' Even if we admit that we pray in this
fashion, I do not believe that we can do so all the time.
Yet there is another, interior kind of prayer without
ceasing, namely, the desire of the heart. Whatever else
you may be doing, if you but fix your desire on God's
Sabbath rest, your prayer will be ceaseless. Therefore,
if you wish to pray without ceasing, do not cease to desire.
The constancy of your desire will itself be the ceaseless
voice of your prayer. And that voice of your prayer will
be silent only when your love ceases. For who are silent?
Those of whom it is said: 'Because evil has abounded,
the love of many will grow cold.' The chilling of love
means that the heart is silent; while burning love is the
outcry of the heart. If your love is without ceasing,
you are crying out always; if you always cry out, you are
always desiring; and if you desire, you are calling to
mind your eternal rest in the Lord.—From a discourse
on the psalms by Saint Augustine

Part Two

CONTEMPLATION

On its part let (the soul) simply, lovingly fix its attention upon God, without specific acts. Let it occupy itself . . . in loving attention, quite simply, as one who opens his eyes and fixes them upon a beloved object.—Saint John of the Cross, *Living Flame of Love, Stanza III, 32*

CHAPTER VII

Enjoying Union with God

All that has been said about prayer up to this point is merely a prelude to contemplation. Vocal prayer, meditation, fervent acts of the will, affective sentiments, inner dialogue with the Lord, purging the mind of guilt, practicing the presence of God—all of these may be labeled religious exercises. They are forms of prayer, each good in its own way, but they are not contemplation. When contemplation begins, the so-called religious exercises cease.

Imagine yourself driving to visit a friend. When you arrive outside his house, you stop the car and get out. You do not drive the car into the living room. All the thoughts and actions involved in driving the car represent the many religious exercises used in arriving at the threshold of God's Presence. Once you arrive, you are better off leaving them behind. With contemplation all thoughts and actions stop. To stop everything may seem like a descent into nothingness, but it is not. The initial feelings of emptiness turn to something sweet and fulfilling. Contemplation is the giving and receiving of love. It is loving God, not because of what He gives, but because of what He is.

Contemplation can be viewed from the perspective of the mind or the heart. As an intellectual action, contemplation is silent inner gazing upon the Lord. All that has been stated in earlier chapters about God's love, His Presence,

His beauty, is apprehended and understood in a flashing intuition. You look at Him and He looks at you, but not with the eyes of the body. It is a spiritual gazing, a wonderful awareness of God's Presence. Contemplation, viewed from the perspective of the heart, is the inflowing and outpouring of love. It is the highest act of love.

To contemplate is to enjoy God in a love relationship. Mind, will and heart fuse into one simple action. It is not a self-conscious act, e.g., "Now I am enjoying God." Quite the opposite. The self becomes lost in the loving. All other prayer techniques or methods tend to emphasize the role of the ego in attaining union with God. But there is no need to strain in acquiring this union. In fact, such efforts are counter-productive. God is always present to the soul. In contemplation, all actions of the mind cease. Even if it is only for a few seconds, the achievement of the contemplative state is an experience of joy, one that will nourish every other action throughout the day.

Webster defines the verb "to enjoy" as follows: to experience the excitement of pleasurable feelings caused by the acquisition or expectation of good; gladness, delight, exultation, exhilaration of spirit. There is a problem in defining spiritual things with words that refer to our physical experience, but all the mystics of the Church did this. There simply are no other words to express spiritual experiences.

We do not do full justice to the concept of contemplation by using Webster's definition, but we have to use human words as a basis for communication, and this is the best we can do. Of course contemplation does not depend on physical excitement or bodily feelings. Spiritual pleasure is a different thing entirely. But both of these pleasures have one thing in common: enjoyment. You do not need a dictionary to know that you are enjoying yourself. You do not need someone to define enjoyment when you slake your thirst with a cold, clear glass of water; nor do you need assistance in defining the joy of loving God. It is a rich spiritual pleasure which comes out of silence and a consciousness of one's union with Divine Love. The Presence we seek is within us. God is Love. Your response is silent and distinctly your own. All you need is your faith and your availability.

Contemplation is not the reward of a life of heroic virtue. It is the consequence of a faith which centers on the knowledge of God's love for you. You are destined for an eternity of heavenly joy in and with the Lord. This is why you were created. When with the help of God you attain heaven, ecstasy will be the normal condition of your being. Life here on earth, if lived properly, is intended to be a prelude to heaven.

Even when caught up in sin the soul is still capable of faith and love. Sins of weakness are not roadblocks. "The just man sins seven times daily." The struggle to be good is on-going, and contemplation is possible for all who seek God with a sincere heart, even for the sinner. You have sufficient knowledge of the need of sorrow for sin, so I will not stress it here. I presume it in you. The Lord does not merely want your time, or your attention, He wants your will. He wants you to submit to His plan for your life. Sorrow for past mistakes is part of that surrender, but you must learn to carry on even though you are far from perfect. The Lord loves you even as you stumble. This is why joy is so possible and so fitting for everyone. You have a vocation to joy; accept it.

There are no steps needed in the act of contemplation per se; all the steps are abandoned. What is needed is the simple desire to love and enjoy God. One either knows, or does not know; one either enjoys, or does not enjoy. My aim is to elevate your aspirations to the point where you will see the marvelous possibilities for a happier life in God. Instead of worrying about the worthiness or orthodoxy of your prayer, instead of stewing over your failure to be perfect, think positively. Turn to a higher level of interaction with God. Believe in His Presence and enjoy Him. He is more pleased when you enjoy Him than when you brood over your unworthiness. Do not blind yourself to His love. When you enjoy God you give Him great glory.

The following may be useful to you in learning to contemplate:

1. Understand that to contemplate is to enjoy God; to enjoy God is to give and receive love.
2. Realize that to enjoy God you must believe deeply that He is *Unchanging Love.*
3. Become more conscious that God's personal union with you has been initiated through His action.
4. Appreciate the fact that this union does not depend so much on *your* love for Him, as it does on *His* love for you. No one is worthy.
5. Remember feelings are not facts, even if you do not feel His love or His nearness, His love is within you.
6. To enjoy God you do not need to spend your energy trying to acquire union with Him; simply advert gratefully to His loving union with you and take pleasure in Him.
7. To enjoy God you do not need to depend on words, symbols or actions; you simply gaze upon the Lord in delight.
8. To contemplate is to love God and to receive interior, spiritual pleasure because of your knowledge of His love for you.

Man's highest purpose is to give glory to God. There is no greater glory you can give God than to appreciate His love and believe in His power to unite with you in spite of your unworthiness. You respond to the realization of this union by welcoming Him with a joyful heart. At the end of this time of silent prayer the soul is refreshed and renewed, made ready to take up the duties of life. The effects of contemplation will eventually pervade and permeate your daily life.

Just knowing that you are made to enjoy God can change the direction of your thinking. You will want to live in the presence of God and enjoy all the aspects of the life He gives you: walking, resting, working, playing— all of life becomes infused with His loving care.

Christian happiness is a grave happiness. It is not and cannot be a superficial sense of well-being. We are not talking about a feeling of physical comfort, a well-fed stomach or a contented disposition. Catherine deVinck captures the idea perfectly:

> When we are centered in Jesus Christ, when we know
> that we live in Him and with Him and through Him,
> we experience joy. Yet, our joy, our happiness is a grave
> happiness. For we cannot forget that suffering is very
> much part of our earthly existence. The cross of Jesus
> Christ is a reality which is in evidence in every life.
> Even though we do rejoice in the Lord, we are always
> aware of pain, our own, yet, but in an equally intense
> way, the pain of our brothers and sisters throughout
> the world. Jesus Christ is risen in glory, but He is also
> "in agony until the end of the world." Before His passion
> Jesus said to His disciples, "Ask and you will receive
> so your joy will be full."
> The Christian asks, he receives, he experiences the joy
> of the Lord, a joy rich and full but which is grave:
> here on earth we participate in the mystery of Christ's
> passion and death, we suffer it in our own flesh, we
> know the meaning of tears.*

*(Taken from unpublished notes)

While we can speak of our happiness as a grave happiness we know that the tears will be wiped away and we relate to the essential unchanging happiness of God which is our destiny and fulfillment. God's interior happiness is called his beatitude. Saint Thomas Aquinas calls it the "perfect good of an intellectual nature which is capable of knowing that it has a plentitude of the good it possesses" (*Summa Theologica* I, Q. 26, a.1.). It is God's very nature in us which communicates the fullness of joy to us, while at the same time we live in solidarity with the sinful human family and experience with Christ the painful knowledge that injustice and misery abound all around us.

CHAPTER VIII

A Path to Contemplation

For those who may have difficulty contemplating, remember my earlier advice: Good prayer does not depend on good feelings. The object of contemplation is God, not good feelings. Begin with a prayer disposing your mind and heart to accept God's Almighty Will. Drift deeper into the knowledge of God's Loving Presence. Repeat the name Jesus slowly. Push all thought aside gently. If you find yourself still unable to achieve your goal, do not be anxious. Return to scripture, preferably the words of Jesus. Reading Sacred Scripture is listening to God. The conversation can be rich and satisfying, full of splendor and holiness. Though it is not yet contemplation, which transcends words, it often leads to it.

Here, then, is one suggested technique for enjoying the Lord in contemplation:

1. For about five minutes, meditate on the prayer of Cardinal Mercier. Enter within yourself and speak to the Divine Spirit within you:

> O Holy Spirit, Soul of my soul,
> I adore Thee.
> Guide me, strengthen me, console me.

Tell me what to do, give me
Thy orders,
And I promise to submit
To whatever You desire of me
And to accept everything
You allow to happen to me.
Let me only know Thy will.

2. Be still and know that God is ministering to you with
   love; consoling, strengthening and purifying you.
3. Enjoy.

If distractions persist, turn gently to the name of Jesus
as a kind of Mantra. Receive Him into your heart. Return
again to silence and enjoy the Lord.

There are many books which carry texts of scripture
to fit all moods and all occasions. These should be explored
and used during times of meditation. The following texts
might serve as a stimulant to prayerful dialogue, or a
prelude to contemplation. Remember these lines presuppose
a loving God who is present to you in your trials and
tribulations. Receive His love as you converse with Him.
The sweetness of Jesus is a soft love, but the sternness of
Jesus is a hard love. It is often like the love of a mother
who tries to train her youngsters not to cross the street
alone. The scolding is a loving expression of deep concern,
as though to say, "I care more for your own safety than
you do. Wake up to my warning and you will be safe."

Listen to the *Words of Jesus.**

1. *Anger:* "If then you bring your gift to the altar, and
   there remember your brother has something against
   you, leave your gift before the altar: go first and be

* *The Words of Jesus* (Alleluia Press, Allendale, N. J., 1977).

reconciled with your brother, and then come back and offer your gift." (Matt. 5:22-23)

2. *Avarice:* "Look out and be careful not to be greedy, for even a rich man's life is not assured by his possessions." (Luke 12:15)

3. *Childlikeness:* "Whoever makes himself as small as this child will be the greatest in the kingdom of heaven. And whoever receives in my name a small child such as this one, receives me." (Matt. 18:4-5)

"Amen, I tell you, whoever fails to receive God's kingdom in a childlike spirit shall not enter into it." (Mark 10:15)

4. *Concern for Livelihood:* "That is why I am warning you: Don't be concerned about your survival, what you will eat and what you will drink, nor about your body, what you will wear. Isn't life more than food, and the body more than clothing?" "Don't worry then about tomorrow: tomorrow will worry about its problems. Each day has enough of its own troubles." (Matt. 6:25, 34)

5. *Confidence in God:* "I am the good shepherd: I know my sheep and my sheep know me—as the Father knows me and I know the Father—and I surrender my life in service to my sheep." (John 10:14, 15)

6. *Consolation:* "Let not your hearts be troubled, believe in God and believe in me. In my Father's house there are many mansions, otherwise would I have told you that I was going to prepare a place for you? And when I will have gone and prepared a place for you, I will come back and take you with me, so that you can be where I am. And you know where I am going, and you know the way." (John 14:1-4)

7. *Courage:* "Before my Father who is in heaven, I will

stand by anyone who stood by me in the face of men."

"And when they drag you into synagogues, before magistrates and authorities, don't worry about how you will answer or what you will say: for at that hour the Holy Spirit will teach you what to say." (Luke 12: 8, 11, 12)

8. *Doubts:* "For God so loved the world that He gave His only begotten Son, that everyone who believes in Him may not die, but have eternal life. For God did not send His Son into the world to condemn the world, but that the world may be saved through Him." (John 3:16-17)

9. *Faith:* "Whoever believes in me believes not in me, but in the one who sent me; and whoever sees me, sees the one who sent me. I have come as light to the world, so no one who believes in me is left in the dark." (John 12:44-46)

"If you had faith even like a mustard seed, you would say to this mulberry tree, 'Pull up your roots and plant yourself in the sea,' and it would obey you." (Luke 17:5)

10. *Forgiveness:* "Indeed, I tell you everything you bind on earth shall be bound in heaven, and everything you loose on earth shall be loosed in heaven." (Matt. 18:18)

11. *Freedom:* "If you stand firm in my teaching, you will be my true disciples. You will know the truth and the truth shall make you free." (John 8:31-32)

12. *Fear:* "As for you, all the hairs of your head are counted. Have no fear, then: you are worth more than many sparrows." (Luke 12:7)

13. *Hope:* "I am the Way and the Truth and the Life. No one comes to the Father except through me." (John 14:6)

    "I am not leaving you orphaned: I will come to you. In a short while, the world will no longer see me. But you will see me because I am alive, and you are too. On that day, you will know that I am in my Father, and you are in me, and I am in you." (John 14:18-20)

14. *Humility:* "Anyone who exalts himself shall be humbled, while anyone who humbles himself shall be exalted." (Luke 14:11)

    "Amen, I tell you, the servant is not greater than his master, nor is the messenger greater than the one who sent him. If you know these things, blessed will you be when you practice them." (John 13:16-17)

15. *Hypocrisy:* "Judge not, so as not to be judged. For you shall be weighed by your own judgment and measured by your own standard. Why do you notice the sliver in your brother's eye and not the log in your own? How can you say to your brother, 'Let me remove the sliver from your eye,' while you have a log in your own? Hypocrite! First get rid of the log in your eye, and then you shall see well enough to remove the sliver from your brother's." (Matt. 7:1-5)

16. *Inner Light:* "No one lights a lamp to hide it in a corner or under a basket: he places it on a stand, so that those who come in may see it. The eye is the light of the body. When your eye is whole, your entire body is full of light. When it is bad, your entire body is in darkness. See to it, then, that the light in you be

not darkness. For if your body is entirely luminous, without any dark area, it shall be as entirely clear as when a bolt of lightning shines upon you." (Luke 11:33-36)

17. *Love:* "Love the Lord your God with all your heart and with all your soul and with all your intelligence. This is the great and first commandment. And the second is similar to it: You shall love your neighbor as yourself. On these two commandments depend all the law and the prophets." (Matt. 22:34-40)

"I give you a new commandment: Love one another; as I have loved you, you too love one another. In this shall everyone know you are my disciples, if you have love for one another." (John 13:34-35)

"As the Father loved me, so I loved you: abide in my love. If you keep my commandments, you will abide in my love, as I have kept my Father's command and abide in him." "Greater love no man has than to lay down his life for his friends." (John 15:9, 13)

18. *Needs:* "Ask and it shall be given to you; seek, and you shall find; knock, and it shall be opened to you. For everyone who asks receives, and he who seeks finds, and to him who knocks it shall be opened." (Matt. 7:7-8)

19. *Peace:* "I leave you my peace, I make you a gift of my peace. Not as the world gives do I give to you. Let not your hearts be troubled or afraid." (John 15:27)

"And you therefore have sorrow now; but I will see you again, and your heart shall rejoice, and your joy no one shall take away from you." (John 16:22)

20. *Persecution:* "Blessed are those who are persecuted for justice' sake, for theirs is the kingdom of heaven. Blessed are you when men revile you and persecute you and falsely accuse you of all kind of evil because of me. Be glad and rejoice, for your reward is great in heaven: for so did they persecute the prophets before you." (Matt. 5:10-12)

21. *Prayer:* "When you pray, go into your room, close your door, and pray to your Father in secret, and your Father who penetrates secrets, will reward you openly." (Matt. 6:6)

"Which one of you, indeed, if he asks his father for bread will be given a stone, or if he asks for a fish will be given a snake, or again, if he asks for an egg will be given a scorpion? If, then, you who are wicked can give good things to your children, how much more evidently shall your Father in heaven give a spirit of holiness to those who ask him?" (Luke 11:11-13)

"Again I tell you, if two of you ask together for anything on earth, it shall be given to them by my Father who is in heaven: for when two or three come together in my name, I am there in their midst." (Matt. 18:19-20)

22. *Pride:* "The greatest one among you shall become your servant. Whoever exalts himself shall be humbled, but whoever humbles himself shall be exalted." (Matt. 23:11-12)

23. *Resignation:* "My Father, if possible, let this chalice pass me by; yet, be it not my will, but yours." (Matt. 26:39)

24. *Revenge:* "You have heard it was said: An eye for an eye, a tooth for a tooth. But I tell you: do not resist a wicked man. On the contrary, if anyone strikes you

on the right cheek, turn also the other to him; and if anyone sues you and takes your shirt, let him also take your coat; and if anyone forces you to walk one mile with him, walk two miles instead. Give to the man who begs from you, and turn not away from the one who would borrow." (Matt. 5:38-42)

25. *Scandal:* "Woe to the world for being the occasion of scandal! Some such occasions cannot be avoided: but woe to the man through whom they come. And so, if your hand or foot is for you an occasion of scandal, cut it off and throw it away: it is better for you to enter life with one hand or one foot than to be cast into eternal fire with both hands and both feet. And if thy eye is occasion of sin to thee, pluck it out and throw it away; it is better for you to enter life with one eye than to be cast into hell-fire with both eyes." (Matt. 18:7-9)

26. *Tiredness:* "Come to me, all you who labor and are heavily burdened, and I will give you rest. Take my yoke upon you, and learn from me: for I am gentle and accessible, *and you shall find relief for your souls;* for my yoke is easy and my burden light." (Matt. 11:28-30)

27. *Union with Christ:* "I am the true vine, and my Father is the vine-tender. Every barren twig in me he prunes, and every fruitful one he trims to increase its yield. Now, you are already pure because of the words I have spoken to you: remain in me as I will in you. As a branch cannot bear fruit on its own, but must remain on the vine, neither can you unless you abide in me. I am the vine, you are the branches. He who abides in me, and I in him, he is the one who bears much fruit; for without me you can do nothing." (John 15:1-5)

28. *Watchfulness:* "You, too, be ready, for the Son of Man will come at an hour you don't expect." "For much will be demanded of a man who has received a lot, and more will be expected of a man to whom more things have been entrusted." (Luke 12:40, 48)

29. *Wisdom:* "Beware of false prophets who come to you in sheep's clothing, but are ravenous wolves within. You shall know them by their fruits. . . . For every good tree produces good fruit, while the bad tree produces bad fruit. A good tree cannot produce bad fruit, nor can a bad tree produce good fruit." "Everyone, then, who hears these words of mine and acts upon them I will compare him to a wise man who built his house on rock and the rain fell, and the torrents came, and the winds blew and battered that house, but it did not fall, because it was founded on rock." (Matt. 7:15-20; 24-25)

Conclusion

Some bright and happy souls enjoy the Lord all the time. They radiate joy. Others seem to feel this joy only on occasion. Some feel entirely deprived of joy. If you are among the latter, don't be discouraged. It will pass. You are not abandoned in your pursuit of an invisible, unattainable God. He is in love with you; He is pursuing you. Your joy in Him is yet to be discovered. He will ignite the fires of your heart in time. Perhaps a veil is there for some reason unknown to you now. Do not fear, it will be lifted.

Neither should you be afraid of your weakness, your blindness. The supreme hope of Christians is not in self, but in God. "With God all things are possible."

Try not to fall into the trap of thinking that you can achieve contemplation by sheer will power. You cannot produce joyful feelings on command. We have all seen the plastic smiles that mask a contrived cheerfulness. There's no use trying to show it off before you have it. Just be calm. God's interior happiness is as close to you as your own heartbeat. It will overcome all obstacles and penetrate every layer of pain and bitterness if you allow it.

Becoming like a child, entering into the world of God's joy, is possible for you, if you ask. He has promised it. It will come to you, perhaps when you are tired of asking or when you least expect it. It may be mingled with the pain of life, but you will know when it comes.

The embrace of love, whether you feel it or not, is not a future gift. It is present to you here and now. God is Unchanging Love. He is with you, the same today, tomorrow and always. In time it will become clearer for you and for me. When it does, our joy will be full.